STANDING IN THE BLAZING LIGHT OF GOD

Thoughts & Stories Of A Modern Rabbi

By Rabbi Gary M. Spero, J.D.

Table of Contents

Acknowledgements	2
Preface	4
Chapter One – Growing up Litvak, Embracing Mysticism As an Adult	9
Chapter Two – The Message About My Brother Mark	12
Chapter Three – The Bible Contest And The Truth About Demons	14
Chapter Four – Judaism On Angels And Demons	18
Chapter Five – What Is The Structure Of A Jewish Prayer Service?	22
Chapter Six – Helping The Less Fortunate, Tzedakah Versus Charity	29
Chapter Seven – My Advice On Dealing With Loss And Grief	31
Chapter Eight – Elements Of A Jewish Wedding	38
Chapter Nine – Jewish Death, Funeral And Mourning Rituals	45
Chapter Ten – Adding Holiness To The World Through Actions And Words	51
Chapter Eleven – There Are No Saints In Judaism, We All Have Our Flaws	53
Chapter Twelve – Conversations With Father Luke Dyjak	59
Chapter Thirteen – A Word About Translations Versus Original Texts	61
Chapter Fourteen – The Story Of How We Obtained A Very Old Torah Scroll – The Native American Casino Miracle	63
Chapter Fifteen – What Is The Purpose And Meaning Of Life?	65
Chapter Sixteen – Are All Religious Paths Equally Valid?	71
Chapter Seventeen - My Ideal House Of God	73
Chapter Eighteen - Including Animals In Our Spiritual Lives	75
Chapter Nineteen - The Most Challenging Part Of Scripture, Judges Chapter 11	83
Chapter Twenty – Lessons I Have Learned From Others	85
Chapter Twenty One – Stories and Lessons I Have Learned From My Family	88
Chapter Twenty Two - My Mom's Recipe For Chicken Matzo Ball Soup a.k.a. Jewish Penicillin	101
Chapter Twenty Three – Our Bashert Moment, Meeting And Marrying Sheryl Lynn Joiner, The Love Of My Life	104
Chapter Twenty Four – Does The Body Sin Or The Soul?	109
Chapter Twenty Five – What Is The Reason for The Jewish Star?	111
Chapter Twenty Six – A Few Words About Some Congregants	112
Chapter Twenty Seven – Some Weird Rabbi Stories From Over The Years	114
Chapter Twenty Eight – The Hardest And Most Joyous Days In My Rabbinic Work	119
Chapter Twenty Nine - What Does Judaism Say About Various Issues?	122
Chapter Thirty – Do Jews Believe In An End Times Scenario?	130
Chapter Thirty One - What Is The Jewish Calendar And Why Are Mondays So Difficult?	132
Chapter Thirty Two – Why Do Jews Circumcise Their Males And What About Converting to Judaism?	148
Chapter Thirty Three – Closing Thoughts And Why I Learned To Ride A Harley Davidson Motorcycle	151

Acknowledgements

For many years I have been teaching about Judaism and have learned much as a student and in my work as a Rabbi. I thought it would be good to write these things down to share with others. At age 49 I have undergone some significant health challenges. It occurred to me that if, God forbid, I am not alive when my kids grow up, I would like them to know about my beliefs and teachings.

This summer, while my family is visiting my in-laws in Texas, I wanted to take the time to complete this book.

My sincerest thanks go out to my smart and lovely wife Sheryl for her editing input and suggestions of the subjects covered. You are truly the love of my life.

To my dear friend and Congregant, Joanie Shulman, a retired English teacher, thank you for correcting my punctuation and grammar! Thank you for your support and encouragement in making this book a reality. School teachers rock!!

My thanks to Dr. Mona Bloom for finding additional errors both Joanie and I missed.

I also want to thank my best friend Menashe Cohen, the *Gaon v'Ilui* (sage and genius) who has known me since we were 14, and who made some great suggestions on topics to include in this book.

I hope it will be of interest both to Jews and non-Jews alike. I want to thank my children, Esther Rose Spero and James Robert Spero, my "Jim Bob", for giving me the incentive to write this book. May you both grow up to be healthy, happy and wiser than your old man.

My thanks go to my congregants and the local interfaith community who have enriched my life beyond measure.

I want to thank Dr. Homer Boyd, M.D. for his Torah questions and our email theology discussions. Also for flying my Mom and I through downtown L.A. one time in his helicopter without doors!

Thank you, dear reader, for your time and for purchasing the book. My thanks go to God for keeping me alive and well to reach this joyous moment.

Rabbi Gary Spero

Preface – The Night I Saw God

I was alone in a small, cheap hotel room in New York City's Upper West Side on the night of June 18th, 2003 when I saw God. The hotel was an old one and the room had bizarre steps and dips on the linoleum clad floor.

After 38 years of studying Judaism, learning ancient Hebrew and Aramaic texts and prayers, I had successfully completed the final 3 days of tests and discussions with the *Beit Din*, the Rabbinical Court, and would receive my ordination as a Rabbi, my *Semicha*, the following night. *Semicha* is an old Hebrew word meaning to press on the head with hands. Every Rabbi from Moses ordaining his student Joshua, up until the present day, receives a blessing while their teacher places his hands on the student's head. Interestingly enough, the ancient *Cohanim*, the Priests descended from Moses' brother Aaron, would lay their hands on a sacrificial animal the same way before slaughtering it and offering it to God.

My wife Sheryl and my mother Pearl were back home in Torrance, CA. I had called them earlier in the day to let them know the good news that I had passed my final tests. They were scrambling to make flight arrangements from Los Angeles to New York. They would attend the ordination ceremony the following night in Manhattan's Lower East Side. In the late 1800's and early 20th century this area was the hub of Judaism in New York. Some of my ancestors lived there after making it through Ellis Island from their old homes in Lithuania and Russia.

Growing up I loved spending time with my grandmother Esther who lived with my parents for many years. As a young boy I would climb into her bed on many early mornings. She would often give me a kiss and bless me in *Yiddish*, an eastern European Jewish language. She would say: '*A Brocha On Dein*

Kopf – 'A blessing on your head.'

After my grandfather Nathan's untimely death in 1942, she raised my mother Pearl and my Uncle Lou by herself while running a small general market in Astoria, Long Island. My grandmother's death in 1982 had left me shattered. She was 92, I was 17 and we were very close. It was the first time death had really touched me.

On the night before my ordination, my primary teacher and ordaining rabbi, Rabbi Joseph H. Gelberman, of blessed memory, gave me instructions to prepare myself for the ordination. He had received these instructions some sixty-five years earlier from his ordaining Rabbi.

He told me to immerse myself in a Jewish ritual bath, called a *mikveh*. I should then make a full confession to God of my sins and failings and identify any aspects of my life up until that time which I didn't want to bring with me into my new life as a Rabbi. He told me to do the *Viddui* prayer, recited by the dying, and specifically to tell God that I was open to receiving any messages God would want to send me. I did these things and went to sleep at about 11:00pm. I was completely unprepared for what would happen.

My experience was so intense and so vivid that I cannot call it a dream. I remember in complete detail every aspect of what happened, unlike my dreams, which usually fade away quickly upon waking.

In this experience I awoke as a young boy of four or five in my old bedroom at my parent's house in Torrance. The house was dark and I was wearing child's pajamas with the feet attached. I had my adult mind in this young version of myself. I opened the bedroom door and stepped into the hallway. All was dark and quiet. I walked to the room my Grandmother Esther Lunsky, of blessed memory, used to sleep in across from my bedroom.

I grasped the doorknob and opened the door. I stepped into

the room and saw the merest outline of the room I remembered. Her bed and the hanging lamp above it were present as was her dresser and mirror. The floors and walls were transparent. Most unusual was that I could see a covered form lying in her bed, but not my grandmother herself. Normally when I dream of my grandmother I see her as I knew her in life, a kind, loving, elderly woman with a beautiful full head of white hair.

From the windows on the eastern wall of the room an amazingly brilliant and silent Golden Orange light started to flood the room. The color was so intense, like the hue of a late autumn California sunset. The light was pulsating, emanating white streamers of light in all directions.

When these streamers of light contacted me they passed through me with an incredible and overwhelming sensation of joy of an intensity I have never known in life. It was like standing in the middle of a blazing incandescent bulb, thousands of times brighter than the sun. The light did not hurt my eyes to look at it. When a streamer of light passed through me it was comparable to being run over by an immense locomotive train made of pure and intense joy. And then I heard my grandmother's voice come from the light saying 'A brocha on dein kopf' – 'A blessing on your head' in Yiddish. I knew that this was not just my grandmother's soul speaking to me, but something immensely more. My grandmother was a part of that Voice and it spoke to me using the gentle touch of my grandmother's voice. I looked upward into the midst of that great blazing light and began to run with all my strength into it, wanting to merge with it. I was thrown into absolute blackness and immediately became aware that I was conscious, awake, trembling, shaking and crying in the hotel room. It was 2:00 a.m. I don't know how long the experience had lasted in 'real' time.

My suspicion is that if a person had been in the room with me, they would have viewed me as dead while it lasted. I knew that I had heard the Voice of God and stood in God's blazing golden orange light. Not just the Jewish concept of God, but the God

of everything in the Universe including all humanity and
whatever lives in all of the galaxies. Emotionally I was floored.
I had no idea that the ritual I had followed would bring on
such an intense message. It would be years before I could
speak of this without trembling and becoming emotional.

When I met with Rabbi Gelberman and my seminary
classmates the following day I was still feeling overwhelmed
and trembling.

I could barely speak of my experience. One of my classmates,
a professional hypnotherapist, offered to try and put me under
to relate it. I agreed and was able to convey what had
happened. Rabbi Gelberman told me I should dance with joy
as God spoke to me using my grandmother's touch. This
experience profoundly changed my life and my view of religion,
life after death and spirituality.

Rabbi Bernie King, of blessed memory, told me that the words
'A blessing on your head' are significant since that is where
the blessing of ordination is given.

In the decade following, I would help many congregants and
their families through death, grief, and loss. My congregation
was an older one and many of our founding members from the
1940's were still active in synagogue life. Over the course of
ten years we had funerals for 28 families, nearly half of the
congregation. Because of my pre-ordination experience I had
no doubt whatsoever that God exists and is personally
involved with our lives. I know that our souls continue on after
death in absolute joy as we merge with God's eternal light. As
Rabbi Gelberman had taught, I had no doubt that God's
complete message to mankind was given in numerous forms.
We should study and appreciate it all to understand the
totality of that message.

I teach my students that all of the world's great faiths transmit
deep absolute truth. In my home there are many varied light
switchplates on the walls of the rooms. Some have a Kokopelli
figure, others a Siamese cat, some are blank white. The same

electricity flows to each of them even though they look different from each other. So, too, there are many roads to the Eternal. My path goes through Mount Sinai. For others the route might be through the Hills of Galilee, the Ganges River or Mecca. They may differ in language, appearance and ritual approach. The same blazing light of God's Eternal Spirit flows to each.

I love interfaith gatherings where we can praise God in our varied ways together. Like a great choir where various voices combine for a deeper harmony than any of the individual components could achieve alone, so, too, we magnify our spirituality when we join together in prayer and study.

CHAPTER ONE - GROWING UP LITVAK, EMBRACING MYSTICISM AS AN ADULT.

Among Jews of Eastern European descent, called Ashkenazim, there are two distinct groups, Litvaks, (Lithuanian Jews), and Galitzianer Jews from everywhere else in Eastern Europe. They spoke Yiddish with different dialects and had very different views on how to be a Jew.

Litvaks had their own *yeshivot*, schools of study, that focused sharply on Jewish law and the practical aspects of Judaism. Mysticism and spiritual commentaries on Judaism were downplayed if not altogether ignored.

European Judaism had a huge change under Rabbi Yisrael Ben Eliezer, born in 1698 in Podolia. In the 18th century, he gained reknown as a powerful charismatic Rabbi called the *Baal Shem Tov* (literally the Master of a Good Name). He taught what would become Hasidic Judaism with enormous followings. The Hasidic movement recognized that not everyone could sit in the yeshiva all day studying and praying. The Baal Shem Tov taught his disciples that worshipping God with joy, singing and dancing could be just as meritorious as dry discourse and prayer. They created *Nigguns*, wordless melodies, that anyone could sing with an ecstatic heart.

By contrast the Litvak view of Judaism as more of a legal contract with God made them seem like cold fish to the Hasidim. The divide between these two approaches was so great that disdain existed, and still exists, and, at times in the past violence erupted.

My grandfather Nathan Lunsky was raised and trained in the yeshiva of Skidel, Lithuania. The mystical tradition of interpreting the Torah referred to as Kabbalah was not part of his training. He studied the ancient texts with a lawyerlike approach. During the Depression my Mom as a girl would keep him company in his store. He would hand her the daily paper, pick out a news item and make her argue both sides of the dispute, the way he learned Talmud in Skidel. Although I never knew my grandfather, his method of study is what I learned. Go over every aspect of the ancient texts and commentaries weighing the validity of differing points of view. Mysticism and spirituality were not something to which I gave much thought. Concepts such as the soul continuing after death and what our purpose is in life were not the focus of my belief or studies.

My wife Sheryl and I had only one heated argument in the 12 years we have known each other. While dating, Sheryl asked me if I believed in the soul continuing to exist after we die. I told her I didn't know, but hoped so. Wrong answer! We then talked about the differences in the approach to faith held by both the Pharisees and Sadducees in ancient Israel. The Pharisees created Rabbinic Judaism, by building fences around the main precepts in the Torah, while the Sadducees took the text more literally. For example, the Torah states 'You shall not boil a kid in its mother's milk' (Exodus 23:19). In ancient times dairy and meat cattle were often kept together in small herds. The use of a dairy product from the mother to prepare the veal from a calf was a likely possibility. The rabbis built fences around that commandment ordering a complete separation of milk and meat dishes. Separate sets of dishes and silverware are used in Kosher homes. Even a chicken breast sandwich cannot be topped with cheese. Chickens don't have nipples and don't feed their babies milk so what is the problem? A person could mistake a raw piece of veal for a raw chicken breast and God forbid put cheese from the mother cow on it.

By contrast the Sadducees, mainly priests descended from Aaron, took the Torah literally and didn't build such fences around the commandments. I told Sheryl that I was more comfortable with the Sadducee approach to life which doesn't really talk of an afterlife but focused more on what to do while living. The afterlife would take care of itself, if there is one.

Sheryl rightly pointed out that if the Sadducees had their way,

Judaism would have died in the year 70 when the second Temple was destroyed by Rome, as animal sacrifice was the Jewish religious practice at the time. Rabbi Yochanan Ben Zakkai, created modern synagogue based Rabbinic Judaism guided by Pharasaic principles after the Temple fell. He saved Judaism from the dust bin of history.

I should have had a more open mind despite being a Litvak. Two events growing up made me aware that something more exists than what we perceive.

Chapter Two - The Message About My Brother Mark

When I was ten years old my older brother Mark joined the Teacher Corps and was sent to Harveyville, Kansas to live and teach.

I visited him there in the summer of 1976 and was struck by the friendliness and closeness of the residents of the small town. One lady was nearly 100 years old and she picked apples from the tree in her yard and baked us a fresh apple pie. Mark established a boy scout troop there and studied and taught in Emporia, Kansas.

He was the first Jewish person to come to the town. It is hard to imagine, but in 1975 some people asked him if it was true that Jews had horns on their head. He allowed them to touch his head to see that there was no truth to that myth. Mark became an accepted and welcomed resident of the town. I missed Mark terribly during his time there. We would talk on the telephone each week. He would send me cassette recordings of "Mystery Theater" that he taped off the local AM radio station and even brought home some pet box turtles for me one time.

One winter night my parents and I spoke with Mark and were happy to hear that all was well. I went to sleep. A few hours later I awoke from a very vivid dream of speaking with a lady who told me to wake my parents as Mark had been in a car wreck but he would be OK.

I immediately ran to my parents insisting that they call Mark. They told me it was probably just a bad dream as we had spoken with Mark a few hours earlier and all was well. I insisted and they called Kansas, despite the late hour. We learned that Mark was driving his Ford Maverick home but swerved sharply to avoid hitting a dog in the road. The road was icy and his car went into a ditch. He was banged up but not seriously injured. I took that experience as a message from an angel.

My mother told me that during WW2, when her father died suddenly and she was 16, she kept having a recurring dream. She would see her older brother, my uncle Dr. Louis Lunsky, standing on the porch carrying his Army duffel bag. He was not expected to come home from Europe where the war was raging. During that week, President Franklin D. Roosevelt ordered that sons who were the sole support of widowed mothers and families be discharged and he indeed came home just as my mother had been dreaming.

The second experience for me at age 17 was even more direct and frightening.

Chapter Three - The Bible Contest and The Truth About Demons

As a product of a Reform Jewish synagogue upbringing, I did not study about angels and demons and would have thought they had no place in modern Judaism. Judaism, as I understood it, was focused on doing acts of kindness and improving our world during our lives. As a teenager I competed in the National Bible Contest for Jewish Youth sponsored by the World Zionist Organization. The contest involved memorizing the Torah, Prophets and Writings that comprise the Hebrew Bible. Jews do not refer to it as the 'Old Testament,' as 'Old' would mean it had been supplanted by something 'New.' We refer to it as the *Tanakh,* the Hebrew acronym for the first five books, the prophets and the writings.

A student would compete in either the English or Hebrew division for the local title. Whoever won locally would travel to New York City for the National Bible Contest. It was a matter of strict memorization. A question might be 'How many times does the word 'go' appear in the Book of Genesis?' The most correct answer would win.

The division winners of the National Bible Contest would travel to Israel to compete in the International Bible Contest for Jewish Youth. The contest is a televised event taking place around Israeli Independence Day every year. I was blessed to have excellent teachers, particularly Mrs. Susie Lipow of Temple Menorah and Rabbi Ben Zion Friedman from Chabad of South Bay who worked tirelessly with me.

In 1981 I won both the Los Angeles and National Bible Contests in my division. I traveled as part of the US team to compete in Israel in April 1982. The contest that year took place in Jerusalem and Netanya, Israel. It was wonderful to meet other kids my age from all over the world and to see the places we had studied about. I traveled with Linda Nulman of Cranston, Rhode Island and it really was a lot of fun. We stayed in an Israeli *Gadna* army camp in Joara, near the Golan Heights in the North of Israel, and explored quite a bit of the country. Hiking the snake trail down from the fortress at Masada was amazing, as was the oasis at Ein-Gedi near the Dead Sea.

Poor Linda got attacked by a psychotic ram that got away from a herd of sheep, but fortunately she wasn't seriously injured.

The overall winner of the contest that year was a 17 year old Israeli genius who had such an amazing memory! A pin could be stuck through five pages of an Aramaic Talmud and he could state each letter it had pierced. I was fortunate to place 10th in the world ranking, and fifth in the Diaspora ranking for Jews living outside of Israel.

When I returned home, I graduated from West High School in Torrance a year early in 1982. Because of my involvement in the Bible Contest, I was offered and accepted a four year full scholarship to Yeshiva University of Los Angeles, a west coast campus of Yeshiva University of New York.

For four years I experienced and lived life as an orthodox Jew. Days would start with morning prayers followed a full day and evening of classes. We broke for breakfast, lunch and dinner, and afternoon and night prayer services. I was actively studying from 8:00am until 11:00pm, except on the Sabbath. My Hebrew and Aramaic knowledge improved greatly. Classes on the Torah, Talmud, Jewish Law and ritual were intensively studied. It was during this time in my life that I learned not to mess with demons. My Talmud teacher would often take our class outside to a garden atrium to study in the mild Los Angeles weather. Studying a page of Talmud is an intense experience. Much of the text is written in Aramaic, an ancient Semitic language similar to Hebrew that was the vernacular in Israel 2000 years ago. The text and commentaries are written very densely in blocks surrounding the central and oldest text, known as the Mishnah. It could take weeks to complete a few pages of Talmud.

When I was 17 our teacher took us out to the atrium to continue studying an ancient text that talked about demons. We had been studying it for many days. The Talmud says that at all times the air around us is filled with thousands of flying entities we cannot see. It is good that man cannot see them as a person would go insane if he could see what was really there. My patience ran out when we had an hour long discussion about the meaning of bird tracks appearing in fireplace ashes. Apparently such tracks could indicate the presence of *shaydim*, demons. My Litvak mind rebelled.

'Why can't we study something practical?' I asked the teacher. 'Teach about Shabbat or Passover, or returning lost items, but why waste time studying this nonsense?' The Rabbi calmly stated that I was free to leave at any time but we would study all of the texts in the volume.

At 17 I thought I knew it all and got up to leave. I only walked a few steps when I heard a very large crash into the palm tree I was passing beneath. A huge, jet black crow had flown beak first into the tree, breaking its neck. Its' twitching body fell just in front of me. Coincidence, I thought, and walked to the parking lot to take a drive in my 1972 Buick LeSabre. The day was very mild and my car was well maintained. About a block from the school my car filled with acrid white smoke. I pulled over and saw the smoke was pouring from the trunk. I popped the trunk and saw my prayer shawl, my *tallit*, in its bag, had spontaneously combusted into flames. The day was not hot and there were no loose wires in the trunk.

The *tallit* bag itself was not burned but the prayer shawl within was on fire and the special knots in the fringes were unknotting themselves. I took my smoldering tallit and returned to class. The Rabbi did not so much as bat an eye but said 'Because of your bad attitude that bird was killed.' He did not seem shocked about the tallit burning up. I never again complained about anything that was taught. The Torah does not say that there is no truth to demons, psychics and fortune-tellers. It just says don't mess with these things and I firmly support that view. As will be discussed later, I believe that true psychics can relate meaningful messages although we are told not to seek them out.

Chapter four - Judaism On Angels and Demons

The Jewish view on angels and demons is different from the Christian view. First it should be noted that in Judaism God alone reigns Supreme over everything. There is no devil, no separate force for evil, which tries to subvert God's Will. There is an angelic figure called the 'Satan' (pronounced Sah-Tahn in Hebrew) who is a sort of Divine prosecuting attorney. When our lives are being judged by God, this Satan points out all of the instances where we could have made better decisions. Other entities point out all of our good deeds and meritorious works. There is no hell in Judaism. People who are evil in their lifetimes might not be allowed to have their souls continue to exist after death. There is a belief in a sort of reincarnation, called a *gilgul*. If a person never learned to work well with others they might be brought back as an ant or a bee, where they have to work with others in the colony or hive.

Angels, called *Malachim,* in Hebrew, are like blank floppy discs or recordable CD's. They are programmed by God to do only one task at a time. They have no free will but do as tasked without question. One day an angel might be dispatched to assist a person, appearing as a normal human being. The next day it might serve as the Angel of Death. Certain angels are given names, such as Michael (meaning Who is Like God?) Raphael (Healer of God) Gabriel (Might of God) and Uriel (Light of God). These beings are eternal and are a way for God, who is pure spirit, to interact with the physical world.

When Joseph went looking to find his brothers, all of Jewish history to come depended on him finding them, but he was having trouble. He met 'A man in a field' who directed him to Dothan where his brothers were located. Tradition says that this was an angel although Joseph did not know it. If he didn't find his brothers, they wouldn't sell him as a slave to a caravan. That meant he would not have been taken to Egypt. If he didn't reach Egypt, he wouldn't be thrown into prison after being falsely accused of rape/assault by Potiphar's wife. If he wasn't in prison he never would have been summoned to Pharoah to interpret Pharoah's dream. If he hadn't interpreted the dream, he would not have risen to be the second to Pharoah to rule over Egypt. He would not have planned out a way to save the harvests for the coming famine and would not have saved his brothers and father from starvation. If Jacob and his sons had not then moved to Egypt to reunite with Joseph, their descendants would not have later been enslaved to subsequent Pharoahs. Had they never been enslaved, there would have been no Moses, no Exodus story, no receiving the Ten Commandments and the Torah at Mount Sinai. No ancient Israel, no Christianity, no Islam.

All of that hinged upon the angel telling Joseph where to find his brothers. Perhaps at times *we too* deliver a needed message to others, with no idea that the history of Western Civilization might depend on our doing just that.

Demons, called *Shaydim*, are also entities that act on behalf of God in a negative way. It is written that they inhabit desolate places and ruins. One should not sleep in such places and should never use a Ouija Board or other means of communicating with them. You will not like what you invite in.

In ancient times there was a Jewish ritual of exorcism for one possessed by a demon. Although not common, the rite of Jewish exorcism continued into modern times. For example, the Jewish community of Nikolsberg in Moravia reports an exorcism in 1696 and again in 1785. The practice continues in very orthodox Jewish communities to this day.

In Jewish literature, demons serve God in their own way. There is a famous story of a second century Rabbi named Shimon Bar Yochai. Rabbi Shimon was a student of the famous Rabbi Akiba. He was a tremendous scholar and mystic who tradition states dictated the *Book of Zohar* on his deathbed. The Zohar is a primary work of Kabbalistic literature.

The Talmud states that Rabbi Shimon was sent to Rome to confront the Emperor and ask him to release the Jews from harsh prohibitions against Jewish practices such as circumcision, and ritual cleanliness. It is said that on the ship to Rome, a demon named either *Ben Temalion* or *Asmodai* appeared to Rabbi Shimon. Rabbi Shimon was disgusted by the appearance of such an entity and asked God: 'To Hagar the Egyptian you sent an angel to assist her and Ishmael but to me you send this thing?' The demon was offended and said 'Don't we all serve God in our way?'

The demon said it would possess the soul of the Roman Emperor's daughter and have her call out Rabbi Shimon's name. The demon stated it would not release the daughter from possession until her father gave in to Rabbi Shimon's demands. According to the story Rabbi Shimon was immediately summoned to see the Emperor upon arrival in Rome. After negotiating a repeal of the restrictions and performing an exorcism the demon released the daughter from its possession. The decree against the Jews was torn up.

Judaism believes that all adults, from the age of thirteen and above are morally responsible for the choices we make in life. If we wrong someone, we much apologize, correct the wrong if possible, and ask forgiveness. If the person wronged refuses three times to give forgiveness, then they have sinned and God will forgive the repentant wrongdoer.

The only exception to this is murder, as the murder victim isn't alive to forgive the killer. Once a year, on *Yom Kippur*, the Day of Atonement, we fast for 24 hours and seek to review our lives and determine how we need to improve. Repentance for bad deeds and a change of heart for the future are part of the liturgy and ritual of that day.

Maimonides, the brilliant Spanish scholar and Rabbi, said that evil does not exist as a separate force in this world. Instead it is like extinguishing a lit candle in an otherwise dark room. One has not created darkness but only removed the light. When we remove the good from our actions, evil is the result. It is hard to understand why good people suffer in a world where God reigns supreme. Tradition states that the **Book of Job**, directly addressing this issue, was written as a teaching tale by Moses himself. Job is described as a righteous person who lost everything, his loved ones, his health and his property, as a test of whether he would curse God. His friends were sure he had committed some great sin and was being punished. Ultimately God rebukes the friends. Job's famous words 'The Lord gives, the Lord takes, may the Name of God ever be praised' are part of the Jewish funeral liturgy.

The conclusion Moses comes to is framed by God's reply to Job, 'Where were you when I created the world?' If we could understand the Mind of God, we would be God. It is an unsatisfying answer to a tremendous question.

A word about the sensation of Déjà vu, that feeling we have been somewhere before that we know intellectually isn't the case. Most people can be summed up in a few words, i.e. she was a kind person, he was a selfish person, a carefree person, etc...

Kabbalah states that parts of our souls which we don't utilize in life are 'recycled' into another person's soul at birth until all of its potential has been realized. Part of your soul might have been in that déjà vu location in a past person's life, triggering the feeling in your own life.

Chapter Five What Is The Structure Of A Jewish Prayer Service?

My late teacher, Rabbi Leon M. Kahane, of blessed memory, taught that Judaism tries to instill in people a desire to live with 'an attitude of gratitude.' Traditional Jews recite over 100 blessings of gratitude and praise for God every day.

Our prayer books, called *Siddurim*, have a very similar structure no matter which form of Judaism is being followed. Orthodox prayer books are virtually identical in Hebrew all over the world. The order of the services has been fixed for many centuries. Hasidic prayer books can vary with the addition of extra words to standard prayers, done for Kabbalistic reasons by various *Rebbes*. (Hasidic Grand Rabbis and leaders) Conservative and Reform prayer books generally have the standard Hebrew texts although they might be shortened or modified to be egalitarian. Most of the Conservative and Reform service will be done in the local vernacular, generally English in the USA, with the addition of numerous Hebrew songs and prayers. The Reconstructionist movement also includes spiritual readings from other faith traditions and is a beautifully written book.

By tradition Jews pray three times per day. This is derived from stories of the Patriarchs and Matriarchs in the Book of Genesis.

Abraham was a morning person. Repeatedly we are told that he 'arose early in the morning' to carry out God's Will. We establish morning prayers through Abraham.

In ancient times the question was asked, 'When is it light enough to be called morning, for purposes of saying morning prayers?' The answer was *'when it is sufficiently light enough to tell blue from white.'* Ancient prayer shawls had a thread of intense blue, dyed from an organ in a sea snail that lives in the Mediterranean Sea, knotted into the otherwise white *tzitzit*, the fringes at the corners.

While in law school I once wrote a paper about how the Roman Empire adopted this as their legal standard too. Have you ever wondered why there are criminal statutes against theft and stronger laws against burglary? Both can involve taking someone else's things. A burglar was defined as *"one who broke and entered into the home of another, at night, with the intention to steal from the homeowner or commit some other felony."*

In ancient times homes were made of mud bricks and burglars would tunnel through a wall to get to the property they wanted to steal, damaging the home. Burglars could be killed on the spot if caught in the act whereas a thief would be tried before a rabbinic court. Why is the burglar killed? Because one who steals at night thinks that people cannot see him and doesn't believe that God sees and judges his actions. His soul may be beyond redemption.

A daytime thief does not necessarily believe that God is unaware of his crime, but may be desperate to get money for food or another necessity. Repentance and becoming a law abiding person might occur.

The Romans, in the Twelve Tables legal code, said that for burglary purposes, morning has broken when a person can tell blue from white. The Roman judges and leaders had a lot of interaction with Rabbis and Jewish courts of law and appear to have adopted the older Biblical standard. This got handed down to the British Common Law and ultimately was adopted by the United States legal system. The power of *Tallit tzitzit!*

Afternoon prayers are attributed to Abraham's son Isaac. The Torah tells us he would go to a field to meditate in the afternoon. His first look at his fiancée Rebecca came while he was praying in the afternoon.

We learn about praying at night from Isaac's son Jacob, later known as Israel (meaning *One who struggles with God*). The vision he had of a great ladder stretching to the heavens occurred at night. Jacob's ladder was interesting in that everyone on it was either ascending or descending. Nothing was still. We learn from this that spiritually we are either growing and ascending, or we are stagnant and descending. There is nothing static about our souls so we should always push ourselves to grow.

I want you to imagine that you are facing a very still pond or lake in the morning. There are no waves and the surface of the water is like glass. If you take a small pebble and cast it into the water, you will see ever expanding circles moving outward from where the pebble dropped into the water. That is the nature of the Jewish morning prayers. We start very focused on ourselves and gradually move outwards until we are Praising God as the Master of the Universe.

It is said by *Kabbalists* (*Kabbalah*, meaning 'that which is received,' is a spiritual/metaphysical commentary and traditions on the Torah) that sleep is 1/60th the experience of death. Each night our souls ascend to heaven to be judged by God on the day that has just passed. For most of us we are granted another day of life and awaken in the morning. For those whose allocation of days has expired, the soul remains in heaven and the body dies in their sleep.

Upon awakening we say the *Modeh Ani* prayer, thanking God for returning our souls to us and letting us awake to a new day. This is the pebble dropping into the cosmic pond.

If we can then get up and go to the bathroom, or otherwise relieve ourselves, we say a prayer of thanks called *Asher Yatzar*, that our bodies are functioning well enough for us to do this. We are grateful that all of our organs and bodily systems are still working. We are grateful that things which should be open in our bodies, such as arteries, are open enough to function. We are grateful that things which should be closed are still closed. We thank God for healing us. These are the first few ripples extending outward. Tradition teaches that if we are only able to move part of one finger, we should still be grateful to God for allowing us to exert some influence on the world and to have the capacity to live a life of meaning.

We say the *Elohai Neshama* prayer, thanking God for giving us pure souls, untainted by any sin, and the ability to be spiritual beings. We are born with pure souls and any 'stains' are put there by our actions and words.

We then move onward to a series of morning blessings. One prayer I love is thanking God for giving roosters the wisdom to know when morning has arrived and to crow aloud so people can start their day. We thank God for making us Jewish, for meeting our needs, for letting us live in freedom, for creating us in God's image, and for crowning Israel with glory. Gradually the prayers continue to expand to being grateful for the world and everything in it and recognizing God's Eternity and Sovereignty over all.

We say the Shma prayer, the central statement of faith in Judaism. '*Shma Yisrael Adonai Eloheynu, Adonai Echad*" meaning *Hear O' Israel, The Lord is our God, The Lord is One.*' We read passages from the Torah commanding us to love the Lord our God with all of our heart, with all of our soul, and with all of our might. We are to do this both in our homes and when we are out and about. We are commanded to teach these things to our children and to hang a section of the Torah in a mezuzah case on the doorposts of our homes. We are commanded to use phylacteries, *Tefillin* in Hebrew, leather boxes and straps placed on our head and arm during morning prayers. These boxes contain sections of the Torah in them.

Curiously the word for the forehead box is in ancient Egyptian and not Hebrew. The word '*Totafot*' (pronounced toe-tah-fote) was an ancient Egyptian word that describes something placed above and between the eyes. Because the commandment to use Tefillin started with the Exodus from Egypt, the Jews at the time used the Egyptian vernacular to describe this item and we still use this word 3,250 years later.

We say the *Barchu* prayer, known as the Call to worship, when we have a *minyan* (Quorum) of 10 adult Jews. The Orthodox only count Jewish men and not women towards a minyan. There are certain prayers we can only say with a minyan, including Mourner's Kaddish, so it is a tremendous mitzvah to be part of a minyan.

The Barchu is done responsively and says *'Praised is the Lord, to whom our praise is due forever' 'Praised be the Lord to whom praise is due now and forever!'*

In 1942-1943 my mother used to go to an Orthodox synagogue every day to say Mourner's Kaddish for her father who died on March 17, 1942. The date happened to be St. Patrick's Day. This became an emotionally hard day for her throughout her life. Ironically my mother died on *Erev Purim*, the start of the Purim holiday (discussed further in the book) on March 3, 2007 and I get the shudders whenever I see the holiday on my calendar each year.

The Orthodox Rabbi at the synagogue she attended did not want to count her towards the minyan. If he could, he would pull men off the street, even non-Jews, to count towards the ten. In absolute desperation he would count two women as one man, which quite rightly offended my mother's sensibilities.

She was often frustrated because the service flew by in Hebrew with no English. She didn't speak or understand much Hebrew. There are several Aramaic kaddish prayers in a service but only one for mourners. The Rabbi would not signal to her when to stand for the mourner's kaddish prayer as he didn't believe a daughter should recite it, but only a son. An old man with a nice white beard took pity on my mother and would signal to her when to stand and say kaddish. She remembered him until her dying day as a kind man who helped her get through that terrible time of grief.

Other prayers include the *Sh'mona Esreh,* meaning 'the 18' (blessings), also called the *Amidah,* meaning standing prayer. It recounts the merits of our ancestors, praises God and requests blessings for our generation.

Other blessings include the *Aleinu,* acknowledging God as being over all mankind and desiring the day when all will bow down and Praise God and *Ein Keloheinu,* a hymn of praise for God. On Shabbat and holidays extra prayers are added. Also on Shabbat and several weekdays the Torah scroll is taken from the ark housing it and read aloud at the assigned reading for the day.

The afternoon and evening services have a similar structure of prayers although they are shorter services.

Jewish prayer books are opened backwards as compared to English books because Hebrew is read from right to left. Most prayer books with translations have the Hebrew and the translation across from each other on the pages. Some prayers are recited while standing, others while seated. The disabled and elderly may sit throughout the entire service if standing is uncomfortable or impossible for them. The main thing is that they are present, a valued part of the congregation.

There are beautiful songs created around the words of the Hebrew prayers. One of the nice things about visiting different synagogues is listening to the various melodies being used. Many synagogues tend to use the same melodies over and over so the congregation will be familiar with them. Some congregations have a Rabbi who leads services. A Cantor, usually ordained men and women who specialize in Jewish ritual music and liturgy may also have this role. Larger congregations often have both a Rabbi and a Cantor. Lay leaders may also lead services. Rabbinic or Cantorial ordination is not required. Some small synagogues only use lay leaders. If you have never been to a synagogue service, feel free to visit your local synagogue. All are welcome and there is no cost to attend.

The one possible exception is during *Rosh Hashana* (New Year) And *Yom Kippur* (Day of Atonement) services in the Fall where seating is at a premium and tickets or membership may be required at many synagogues. There is no weekly 'pass the plate' collection at services.

It is customary to dress up in business attire, or business casual clothing for Shabbat services. Some congregations are very casual and others are not. When visiting for the first time it is better to overdress until you know their custom.

In Orthodox congregations, women have to sit separately from men and should wear a long dress or long skirt paired with a long sleeved conservative/modest blouse. Note that Orthodox men will not shake hands with or touch a woman other than his wife, sister, daughter or other close relative.

This is generally never an issue in Reform or Conservative synagogues and men and women will sit together and participate equally in the services. Virtually all synagogues are welcoming to visitors and there is usually an '*Oneg*' celebration after Shabbat services where people sit around, have some food and socialize.

Chapter Six Helping The Less Fortunate – Tzedakah v. Charity

There is a difference between charity and the Jewish concept of *Tzedakah* (righteous giving). Charity is from the Latin word *'Caritas'* meaning 'from the heart.' If the heart prompts the person to give, he or she will give. If not, they won't. Tzedakah on the other hand is an obligation we have as ordered by God. It doesn't matter whether or not we want to give, as long as we are able to give, we must give. Even the poorest Jews are obligated to give something to those less fortunate than themselves, even if it is a penny.

The Spanish scholar Maimonides, in his work *Mishneh Torah*, detailed the eight levels of giving. On an ascending level, they are as follows:

8. When donations are given grudgingly.

7. When one gives less than he should, but does so cheerfully.

6. When one gives directly to the poor upon being asked.

5. When one gives directly to the poor without being asked.

4. Donations when the recipient is aware of the donor's identity, but the donor still doesn't know the specific identity of the recipient.

3. Donations when the donor is aware to whom the money is being given, but the recipient is unaware of the source.

2. Giving assistance in such a way that the giver and recipient are unknown to each other. Communal funds, administered by responsible people are also in this category.

1. The highest form of charity is to help sustain a person *before* they become impoverished by offering a substantial gift in a dignified manner, or by extending a suitable loan, or by helping them find employment or establish themselves in business so as to make it unnecessary for them to become dependent on others.

This is a major Jewish principle to help others.

Chapter Seven - My Advice On Dealing With Loss and Grief

If one lives long enough, death and grief after losing loved ones and friends is inevitable. The 16th century Roman Catholic mystic, Saint John of the Cross, described the 'Dark Night of the Soul' in a poem, in which we feel isolated from God's light during our spiritual journey. The crushing depression we experience can be overwhelming.

I want to share with you the most difficult time of my life to date, at age 49. Perhaps my way of dealing with the darkness of this period will help you to navigate your journey as well. Growing up I was very, very close to my parents. My mother, Pearl Ann Spero, of blessed memory, in particular had a tremendous impact on my life. She was a good, loving and caring mother. She always tried to be optimistic and retained her faith during a number of terrible life challenges. She had a smile that was very warm and had a caring and listening ear for the problems of others. She had good friends of all ages from numerous religious, racial and cultural paths.

Many years ago she befriended a young Muslim woman named Manijeh who had come to the United States from Tehran, Iran. She would speak and give advice to Manijeh who missed her own mother in Iran. My mother enjoyed watching Manijeh's family grow and often spoke of her as her as her 'adopted' daughter. She had other 'adopted kids' from Catholic, Protestant, Jewish and Buddhist backgrounds as well.

As a teenager my family used to belong to a local swim club with an outdoor pool and Jacuzzi. One man used to sit alone in the Jacuzzi for hours, not speaking to anyone. He had a habit of reading paperback books and tearing out and discarding each page he read. My mother made it a point to say hello to him each day. It took a few years but he started to speak with my mother about his life. One day he tearfully told her that he had served as a Special Forces soldier in the Vietnam War. Many of his friends had died in front of him. He had killed many of the enemy. He was particularly haunted by the death of a buddy who stepped on a land mine directly in front of him. That man's shattered bones tore into his body like shrapnel. He eventually healed from the physical wounds but could not get over the guilt and pain of the things he had done and experienced. My mother reassured him that he was a good person and that war makes us do terrible things to survive. She talked about how my Dad learned to deal with his World War Two combat experiences. They developed a friendship and he started smiling more and seemed more at peace with his life.

After retirement from her career as a bookkeeper, Mom used to make and sell baby quilts at senior citizen art fairs. She always made a few extra from whatever material she could obtain to give to teenaged unwed mothers and others who could not afford baby items but needed them. Her father taught her this during the Depression when he would give the poor whatever they needed from his store even if they couldn't pay.

I learned after her passing that several of my good friends used to call and visit with her regularly to get advice. She had a unique way of relating to others. When I learned to ride motorcycles as an adult (which she was not happy about) I joined a local chapter of the Harley Owner's Group. It was a social club that sponsored and attended charity events, BBQ's and long rides. My folks would often accompany me by car to various Harley Davidson events. It wasn't long before large, bearded and tattooed bikers would rush to hug her and call her Mom. She would sit and give relationship advice to both the men and the women.

After battling a first round with breast cancer, my father's death on November 3, 2005 was very difficult for her. She was not used to living alone after 58 years of marriage. Mom and I would speak on the phone at least 7 times a day. We lived around 6 miles apart and would see each other daily as well. She loved my wife Sheryl like a daughter and was thrilled when we decided to become parents through international adoption. She followed the process closely as we spent months preparing paperwork and working our way through the adoption process. The USA doesn't have orphanages. Court decisions overturning some domestic adoptions made us seek out the international options. Sheryl and I didn't know which country to look to for our children. China had an established program but had very strict health requirements and a waiting period of years. We prayed together for guidance. The very next morning I was talking by telephone with attorney John Hillsman. We had a case together and were opposing counsel. I asked John what was new with him after we talked business. He told me his family just adopted a baby from Vietnam and that the process was very quick. John was God's messenger that day as he put us on the correct path.

We applied to Vietnam and within six months were matched with an infant girl and boy in an orphanage outside of Hanoi. We were 'pregnant on paper!'

Sheryl and I got the telephone call first about our daughter while we were celebrating our fifth wedding anniversary and my Mom's birthday in Solvang, CA. Solvang is a small Danish community in the Santa Ynez Valley of Central California. We were in a Hallmark card store when the call came. We were told that our daughter, named Nguyen Kim Hue, whom we would name Esther after my late grandmother, shared my birthday of May 31st. My Mom said this was a sign from God that all would be well and was meant to be, and broke into tears of joy.

About a week later we received the call about our son, named Le Thai Son. We named him after our late fathers James R. Joiner and Robert Spero. We pored over every photo and detail of their lives that we received. My mother was so excited and happy about becoming a grandmother again, as she loved her granddaughter, Ariana, born years earlier to my older brother Mark and his wife Cindy.

It was during this most joyous time that her breast cancer, which had been in remission for five years, came back with an aggressive vengeance. Through rounds of chemotherapy and radiation she did her best to be cheerful and positive. Many of my congregants and her friends remarked that she did not appear ill. By February 2007 the medical reports became devastating as spots of cancer were invading her bones and organs. She was hoping to live to meet her new grandchildren whom we would be traveling to Vietnam to adopt in mid-March 2007.

By late February her health sharply declined. She requested that a Torah scroll be brought from the synagogue to her bedroom so that she could say a special prayer as she had done when my oldest brother Nathan and my father went through difficult health challenges in years past.

Our synagogue President at that time, Jerry Cohen, rushed to bring a torah scroll to her. I am forever grateful to him for that act of kindness.

I was begging God in my prayers to let her beat back the cancer as she had done once before.

When that wasn't going to happen, I begged God to at least let her meet and hold our soon to be children.

When it became evident that she would die before then, I begged God not to let her suffer.

Mom asked me on the last day she could speak 'What should I be doing?' as she lay in bed. I reassured her that she had lived a full and good life, touching many lives. She should be at peace. She began having vivid dreams of her father visiting her before becoming comatose.

When the end became unbearable I begged God to take her life quickly, peacefully and with love. At 9:00pm on March 3, 2007, 16 months to the day after my Dad's passing, God granted that prayer.

My mother was my congregant and I officiated at her funeral as I had for my father. Who among my colleagues knew her better? My friend Rabbi Ken Giss, also ordained by Rabbi Gelberman, read the eulogy I wrote about her, and Rabbi Mark Hyman led the mourner's kaddish prayer after her burial, which I just could not do.

Sheryl and I could not sit *shiva* for the week after her passing, as is the normal custom. We had to pack quickly and travel to Vietnam. We learned that our son had become ill with pneumonia, which had just taken the life of another infant in the orphanage who was about to be adopted. In America we can get our pets antibiotics without much effort. It was shocking to learn that antibiotics for human babies can be hard to locate in some parts of the world. On the long flight to Vietnam I spoke with Sheryl about my profound sadness that my mother didn't live to meet the babies and how I always thought I could turn to her for advice about learning to be a good father. Sheryl reassured me that together we would learn to be good parents. Sheryl had dreamed of adopting children for many years. I have noticed with other families, that occurrences of death and birth are often nearly simultaneously timed. While this was a time of loss it was also a time of new beginnings for us as a family.

Seven weeks later, when we returned home with our children a congregant's son called me. I did not know him well as he lived out of state, and he had never met my mother. He had a reputation as being a powerful psychic. He told me that someone named 'Pearl' had a message for me. His own mother understood that he was referring to my Mom, Pearl Spero.

He then proceeded to repeat word for word the conversation Sheryl and I had on the flight over to Vietnam. Nobody but Sheryl and I knew of that conversation. He said 'Pearl says not to worry, all will be well with the children.' Although he never had been to our home he described perfectly an archway that separates our kitchen from our family room and told me that is where my mother's spirit watches us feed the kids their bottles. Over the next few months the children would sometimes point and smile at that area although I saw nothing. 18 months later my son saw a photo of my mother and told me he had seen her smiling at them.

The depression and deep grief I felt from Mom's brutal death lasted for years. I did not feel like praising God at times, although there was much to be grateful for. Our wonderful teacher, Rabbi Bernie King, of blessed memory, gave me some advice that really helped me. He asked if I had read the writings of Rabbi Nachman of Breslov, a famed Hasidic Rebbe and student of the Baal Shem Tov. I said that I knew of him but had not studied his writings in real depth. Rabbi King said that when Rabbi Nachman would feel overwhelmed by the sadness in the world around him, he would go to the forest and curse God for the way He was running the world. Rabbi Nachman said 'if you must, go ahead and curse God for 23 hours a day. But in the 24th hour, thank God for whatever blessings remain.' I could be angry and grief stricken while still serving God as a Rabbi and practicing Jew.

The 23rd Psalm gave me quite a bit of comfort as well. King David wrote it to deal with the fear and sadness brought about by death. The English translations do not do justice to the magnificent poetry of the Hebrew.

In particular, most translations say 'Surely goodness and mercy shall *follow me* all of the days of my life.' 'Follow' me is a loose translation of the Hebrew word '*Yeer-deh-foon-ee.*' The Hebrew is much more aggressive than 'follow me.'

It literally means 'will pursue/chase after me.' Indeed the root word '*Rodeph*' is used to describe a murderer in the Bible, who chases someone to strike them down. Yet King David chose that word to describe God's goodness and mercy pursuing after us. I believe this teaches that King David knew that in times of grief and loss we feel isolated from God, perhaps unwilling to praise God.

The Aramaic mourner's kaddish prayer, which doesn't talk of death at all, but rather about praising and glorifying God. Perhaps King David knew that God's mercy and compassion will constantly pursue us, until we are overtaken and can once again acknowledge and feel gratitude and love for God. If we keep saying the words and scrutinize our lives, we will once again eventually regain a sense of peace. The loss of a loved one leaves a void in our lives and a tear in our souls that never completely heals.

I think of grief as coming in waves, like ocean waves. They wash over us and we are helpless to resist the deep sadness they bring. Over time, the waves come less frequently. We learn not to fight them when they come. Acknowledge the loss, cry openly if needed. But also embrace the peace and good memories that will always be with us.

Two of my teachers, Rabbi Leon Kahane, of blessed memory, and Rabbi Joseph H. Gelberman, of blessed memory, survived the Nazi Holocaust. Each lost those dearest to them, their entire families. I asked both of them how can one move forward with life after experiencing such horrors?

Each told me we have two choices in life. Live life with an attitude of gratitude, make something of yourself and build a new family and life, or live life embittered. Those who were embittered and angry often did not live long lives. The sadness and anger consumed them. Those who could rebuild their lives and seek out joy, could have fulfilling good lives despite the terrible pain of loss. It is up to each of us to choose how we go forward.

Rabbi Leon M. Kahane once had an experience that helped further convince me that the soul survives the death of the body. He was at the bedside of a congregant who was about to die. Several weeks earlier the person's younger sister had been killed, but nobody told the dying man as they thought the stress of such bad news would hasten his own demise. After reciting final prayers with the man his final words were 'Rabbi, look, my Papa and Mama are here and my grandparents, but why is my younger sister here? She is alive.' The man passed away with that questioning look of wonder on his face. I take great comfort in knowing that our loved ones wait to greet us when our own time to die arrives.

Chapter Eight -Elements Of A Jewish Wedding

The Talmud tells the story of a Roman matron who was having a discussion with a prominent Rabbi. She asks the question 'What has God been doing since he completed creating the world?' The Rabbi answered 'Making matches between suitable couples.' The Matron thought that was a silly answer and lined up all of her female and male slaves. She randomly picked out couples saying 'You are now married to this one' as she went down the line. The Rabbi came back the next day and saw that the servants were badly bruised and some had broken bones. The Matron admitted that perhaps there is more to making a marriage than two people simply being placed together.

Jews talk about meeting our *Bashert*, our Divinely intended partners. When a couple finds that they are sharing something special and want to continue that relationship permanently, a wedding is the traditional way to accomplish this.

Jewish weddings consist of three major elements dating back to ancient times. While a Rabbi is not needed from a religious perspective to formalize a wedding, modern custom is that the Rabbi officiates at a Jewish wedding. The most ancient way that couples would marry is by entering into a tent or room together unchaperoned with at least two witnesses who see them enter together. If they stay in there alone long enough for 'nature to take its course' they will emerge married. This is preserved today by having couples go together into a room alone after the ceremony for the *'Yichud.'* This gives them 10 minutes or so to decompress with each other before going to the reception. Before my wedding to Sheryl, when I joked with Rabbi Einstein that I would appreciate his clearing off his office desk so we could make full & traditional use of our *Yichud* time together, he moved us to the synagogue library. We behaved ourselves although what better place would there have been to start a marriage to a good looking librarian?

The second element, still used today, is for the groom to give the bride an item worth a dime or more while making a traditional statement. Usually this is a ring exchange done modernly by both spouses. The statement is *'Harei At Mekudeshet Li B'Tabaat Zo K'Dat Moshe v'Yisrael. With this ring you are consecrated to me according to the laws of Moses and Israel.'* If the ring is accepted, the couple is married.

Jewish wedding bands are traditionally a solid band of metal, usually gold, silver or some other precious metal. The ring is not set with stones or otherwise drilled with any openings symbolizing the solidity of the marriage we wish for the couple. Engagement rings may have diamonds or other stones but the wedding band by tradition is simple and unbroken. Orthodox rabbis warn teenagers and younger kids not to play around making this Hebrew statement while handing over an object, as a religious divorce will be required to undo the marriage that will result.

The third method is to write a wedding contract, called a *ketubah*, meaning 'a writing.' This is a legal document, usually written in Aramaic and the local vernacular (English in the USA). It sets out the names of the spouses, the location of the wedding and their intention to marry each other. It also sets forth the terms of the marriage and, God forbid, how to terminate the marriage. Orthodox ketubot give the right to initiate termination to the husband. Egalitarian Ketubot have both partners equal in this regard. Ketubot can be simple forms or elaborate works of art. Couples should spend some time reviewing the type of Ketubah they want and allow time to have it personalized by the artist whose design they select.

I nearly got Sheryl and I thrown out of a Judaica store where we went ketubah shopping before our wedding. Admittedly I have a sense of humor that not everyone always appreciates. There were hundreds of artistic ketubah designs for us to consider. One had a pair of male and female lions sitting next to each other. We both liked cats and were considering this design until I pointed out that the lions had very pained expressions on their faces. I said that I really didn't want to memorialize our love for each other with constipated lions! The shop proprietor nearly tossed me out at that point and was very unhappy. Eventually we found a design we loved by artist Mickie Caspi, and it is proudly displayed in our home.

I recommend to couples that they bring along a plastic poster frame to the wedding. This way they can protect the Ketubah after it is signed, yet allow guests to view it. The ketubah is signed by the couple, the wedding officiant, and by two witnesses. The witnesses are traditionally Jewish, who are not related by blood to either spouse. If the bride doesn't want the groom to see her in her wedding gown before coming down the aisle, each spouse can sign separately. The Ketubah is signed before the actual ceremony.

It is customary for Jewish brides to wear a veil. I like to have the groom lift the veil at the start of the ceremony at the Chuppah and positively ID his bride publicly. I also ask her to confirm that this is whom she intends to marry. When our Patriarch Jacob wanted to marry his Uncle Laban's youngest daughter Rachel he worked seven years for his Uncle for the privilege.

On the wedding night Laban placed a heavy veil over his older daughter Leah's face and hid Rachel somewhere. The couple immediately went to a dark tent to consummate the marriage. In the morning light Jacob discovered he had been tricked into marrying the wrong sister. He had to work another 7 years to marry his beloved Rachel. This caused terrible tension between the sisters and Jacob and started a 'baby birthing war' that resulted in the twelve tribes of Israel plus a daughter Dinah. We Jews never want to get burned by the same trick twice so it is customary to raise the veil and positively identify each other from the outset.

The bride traditionally circles the groom seven times when they arrive at the wedding canopy, called the Chuppah. This is based on a Kabbalistic tradition that there are seven levels to our souls and a wedding knits the seven levels inextricably together. Some couples choose to each circle the other three times with one joint circle together for the 7th. It is a lovely part of the ceremony.

I had an elderly Jewish man ask me once if I knew the real reason for the circling. I gave him the answer stated above. His response was 'No, young man, a vulture always circles the fresh kill seven times before swooping down to eat.' I don't know what it is about marriage disparaging elderly men but virtually every synagogue has one or more in attendance, so be forewarned!

Couples will need a Kiddush cup and some sweet kosher wine for the ceremony. It can be either red or white wine or purple or white grape juice. You will share sips from the cup at two different points in the ceremony. If there is a *tallit*, prayer shawl, special to either spouse, it can be wrapped around both their shoulders during the 7 blessings traditionally recited at Jewish weddings.

I tell couples that this is your day so make sure your wishes are fulfilled by the officiant. If you love a certain poet, reading or piece of music, make it a part of the ceremony. There have been couples who love Star Trek and have done vows in Klingon in addition to Hebrew and English.

I officiated at the wedding of my cousin Sarah and her husband Jeff last Summer and they love Polar Bears. I found a polar bear cap with paws and claws hanging down that I could put my hands into. I used that to bless them in the name of God and polar bears everywhere at the end of the ceremony. People loved that moment more than the rest of the ceremony based on feedback. To couples getting married, it is your day, have fun!

Traditionally the parents, if present, walk each of their children down the aisle. In blended families where everyone gets along, both parents and step-parents can do this as a group. If you have elderly parents or grandparents they can be seated close to the Chuppah in chairs so that they can hear and participate in the ceremony. The chuppah itself can be anything from a simple prayer shawl attached to four tall poles held over the couple by friends, to an elaborate fixed canopy or gazebo. Some couples make their own Chuppah cloths. It symbolizes God being over the couple and the idea of the home you will form.

It is customary for the groom to break a glass object at the end of the ceremony. There are many explanations for this. Some ancient sources say it is to scare off any misfortune that would try to attack the couple. Others say that just as you can never reassemble broken glass to the way it was before being shattered, so too you are making a permanent change in each other by getting married. Some say it is in remembrance of the Second Temple in Jerusalem destroyed in the year 70. Others say in the moment of our greatest joy never forget to be available to assist those with broken lives.

You can designate a person to place the glass object on the ground to be shattered. Make sure their hand is clear before smashing down as injuries have happened carrying out this ritual. Judaica stores sell beautiful thin glass bulbs specifically for this purpose. They come in a special bag to hold the shards. Many of the shards will be multi-colored. A nice idea is to take a transparent *mezuzah* tube and fill it with the shards and a parchment with the appropriate readings to hang in your home's doorway or bedroom doorway. There are also professional companies that can turn the shards into a Kiddush cup or other ritual object.

Jewish weddings differ from Christian weddings in the procession to the Chuppah. Generally all of the groomsmen come down the aisle as a group followed by the best man and the groom with his parents. The bridesmaids come down as a group followed by the maid of honor and the bride with her parents. The maid of honor can gather up a long wedding train and follow behind the bride as she circles the groom. Ring bearers can be used but I suggest tying the rings together with ribbon in a simple bow so that they wont be dropped and roll away at a crucial moment.

In an interfaith ceremony consider using readings from both wedding/cultural/religious traditions. I have added 1st Corinthians on faith, hope, and love to many ceremonies. The vows should be appropriate to each partner. Perhaps a Catholic spouse would rather say I marry you 'according to the laws of the Father, The Son and the Holy Spirit' instead of 'According to the Laws of Moses and Israel.' I have modified the Hebrew ring exchange statement to reflect different wedding traditions. One wedding involved vows in Hebrew, English and Spanish. Make sure your officiant is comfortable with this or find another officiant.

I have heard of some officiants who charge more to do an interfaith wedding since many Rabbis will not officiate. To me this is outrageous. An officiant should have one price for any wedding they undertake. Many clergy will lower or even waive their fee if it puts too much of a financial burden on couples.

In California, marriage licenses are valid for 90 days after issuance. Allow a day to apply for the license as a couple at the county registrar's office. No blood test is required but you have to fill out a form and pay a fee. Remember to bring the license to the ceremony as the officiant can't officially pronounce you legally married without it. The officiant and witnesses will sign it, usually before the Ketubah signing. Designate a friend or the officiant to mail it as soon as possible after the ceremony/reception to the Clerk's office. Pre-pay the postage on the envelope so it may be mailed directly without delay. If, God forbid, either of you should become injured or ill on the honeymoon you will want this license filed so that there is no issue about making medical decisions for each other.

I advise couples to speak with each other before marriage on a number of issues. Do you both want/not want children? If you have a split opinion on the matter really try to work it out before getting married.

If you do want to have or adopt kids, what are your thoughts about raising them with religion and spirituality? For interfaith couples this is crucial because it is far better to teach the kids about both religions in the family and to be respectful of each than to not raise them with anything at all.

Talk about finances. Are you both savers, spenders or divided on the issue? It is usually a good idea for each spouse to have their own individual checking accounts plus a joint account for paying household bills and a savings account for emergencies. It is helpful to give each other access to all accounts so that deposits or withdrawals can be done by either spouse in a crisis.

What are your feelings about pets? Are there allergies or other issues to consider? Does your fiancée have a pet you cant abide? Who will walk the dog, scoop the kitty litter or otherwise provide care? Compromise and putting the interests of your partner and relationship above your own can be important is resolving differences.

One piece of advice my parent's Rabbi gave them in 1947 kept them together until Dad's death 58 years later. If either partner has a very strong desire to do something, and the other partner is neutral or disinclined to do the thing, always give in to the partner with the stronger desire. Never go to bed angry with each other, resolve whatever is at issue first as best you can.

Chapter Nine - Jewish Death, Funeral And Mourning Rituals

If we live long enough, inevitably we will have to deal with death and mourning the loss of friends and relatives.

Traditionally, if capable, the dying person recites the *Viddui* confessional prayer and the Sh'ma prayer. These ask God to forgive them for any times they may have missed the mark in their actions or words. The Sh'ma affirms belief in the One God of Israel.

A rabbi or other person may recite these prayers on the dying person's behalf if needed. I ask the dying if there is anyone they would like to speak with or any relationships they want to try and patch up while there is still time. Ideally a person should be at peace with others and the world before passing. I also like to hear their favorite memories as well as any lifelong regrets they have. If the regrets can be rectified it is good to do so immediately. These conversations can be used with their permission in creating a very personalized eulogy.

When the death occurs, those who are present, or learn of it, say *'Baruch Dayan HaEmet' Praised is the Judge of Truth*. With the exception of on Shabbat, we always try to bury by the next day out of respect for the dead. My grandmother Esther used to say half jokingly 'Check my pulse to make sure before you let them bury me.' The body is taken, washed in a dignified and respectful manner, and traditionally dressed in a simple white shroud called '*tachrichim*.' A person called a *shomer*, will sit up all night with the body reciting from the Book of Psalms.

A Jewish Mortuary can arrange all of this and many use the services of a *Chevra Kadisha*, a Jewish burial society, to do the washing and dressing of the body. Traditionally we do not do embalming and all caskets are closed with no viewing out of respect for the dead. A close relative will look for a moment to make sure their loved one is the person in the casket before the funeral service. The casket by Jewish law is to be a simple wooden box made without nails or metal. Since metal is used to make weapons and things that cause pain, a simple wood casket held together by fitted dowels and joints is the custom. In Israel many times caskets are not used but simply the shroud wrapped body is buried.

In a traditional memorial service Psalms are recited in tribute to the deceased. Perhaps the most famous is the 23rd Psalm. Eulogies are given and the *El Molei Rachamim* memorial prayer is recited. Traditionally a ground burial or mausoleum placement follows. There is a custom for the Pallbearers to pause seven times between the hearse and the grave while certain Psalms are recited. The number seven appears often in Jewish rituals including funerals. It represents the completion of Creation, with God resting for a day after the 6 days of creating the Universe.

There is a custom to lower the casket during the service and for all close relatives (and anyone else who wishes), to place three shovels of soil on the lowered casket. God personally buried Moses after his death, alone but for God, atop a mountain. We too want to do this last kindness for our loved ones, knowing it is a true act of love that cannot be repaid by the deceased. Traditionally each person takes up the shovel for himself, shovels three spadefuls of soil, and then replaces it in the mound for the next person to pick up. The sound of the earth dropping onto the casket is intended to break down any denial of the reality of the death and to start the slow process of healing and acceptance. It is not traditional to have flowers at a Jewish funeral. Often donations to organizations trying to stop the disease or violence that took the life is preferred in lieu of flowers.

It is customary for the family to sit *shiva* for a week after the burial. Shiva is from the Hebrew word Sheva, meaning 'seven.' Traditionally mourners, if physically able, sit on low stools or chairs. Mirrors are covered and mechanical clocks are stopped. A tall shiva candle, given to the family by the mortuary, is lit and will burn for this week. Family and friends bring by lots of food and visit if the mourners are up to receiving them. It is customary not to speak to a mourner unless they address you first and invite speaking. Upon leaving the cemetery we wash our hands. It is customary to have hard boiled eggs at any gathering to represent the circle of life.

We often have Shiva *minyans*, typically afternoon or evening prayer services with at least ten Jewish adults, at the home where shiva is being observed. The mourner's should not have to worry about their appearance or to travel to a synagogue. This allows multiple recitations of Mourner's Kaddish in memory of the deceased. The Kaddish doesn't contain a word about death but are a series of statements of Praise to God. Even though we may not feel like praising God, we say these words until we can say them again with full meaning.

It is customary to study some Torah in their memory at these services. Selections from the Mishnah, the core ideas of the Talmud, are often studied and debated. If you rearrange the Hebrew letters of the word Mishnah it spells Neshama, the Hebrew word for the soul. It is thought that saying Kaddish for the deceased helps propel their souls even closer to God's light than they achieved on their own. We say it for 11 months as none of us wishes to think that our loved one needs a full 12 months of extra merit.

By tradition we place a headstone around a year after the funeral. There is a short twenty minute unveiling ceremony to dedicate the stone. There is a custom to place a pebble or stone on the marker when we visit. In ancient times graves were cairns of stones and this helped to build up and maintain the cairn. We also refer to God as '*HaTzoor*' meaning 'the Rock.' It is a visualization of God as One who is strong, impenetrable, and able to weather any storm. Placing a pebble on the gravestone reminds us of this.

Mourners such as very close relatives will wear a black *Kriyah* ribbon the first week. In ancient times it was customary to rend ones clothing for the dead. This was an improvement over the common ancient custom of slashing oneself with a knife or getting tattooed for the dead. Modernly we tear a black ribbon attached to a button pin and wear it on our clothes rather than tearing a garment.

I love this reading and use it to close all funerals at which I officiate:

We Remember Them by Sylvan Kamens & Rabbi Jack Riemer

At the rising sun and at its going down; We remember them. At the blowing of the wind and in the chill of winter; We remember them.

At the opening of the buds and in the rebirth of spring; We remember them.

At the blueness of the skies and in the warmth of summer; We remember them.

At the rustling of the leaves and in the beauty of the autumn; We remember them.

At the beginning of the year and when it ends; We remember them.

As long as we live, they too will live, for they are now a part of us as We remember them.

When we are weary and in need of strength; We remember them.

When we are lost and sick at heart; We remember them.

When we have decisions that are difficult to make; We remember them.

When we have joy we crave to share; We remember them.

When we have achievements that are based on theirs; We

remember them.

For as long as we live, they too will live, for they are now a part of us as, We remember them.

After a death and funeral give yourself time to heal. The Shiva period is not meant to be a food and drink social party where the mourners entertain the guests. Who could possibly do that after having a painful loss? It is a time for mourning where visitors bring food so the mourners don't have to cook for themselves. It is not a place for levity but rather a time to share memories of the deceased and to comfort the mourners.

Some only sit shiva for an abbreviated three days. The weeklong custom is better and allows for more reflection on the loss and moving forward. I encourage grief support group attendance, and if needed, having your doctor prescribe medication to help with sleeping and dealing with profound grief.

If you have been a caregiver for a prolonged period of time, the difficulty of the loss can be more intense. You may catch yourself thinking 'I need to hurry and prepare a meal for them' or 'It is time for medication to be given.' Following the death you will be instantly transitioned from a very regimented and emotionally draining existence to a life that is suddenly wide open without strict schedules. This can be quite a difficult adjustment.

Be comforted knowing that eventually the memories of sickness and final days will fade to be replaced by memories from better times that will always endure. Try not to visit to the cemetery more than once a month or so and tradition says to stay away for the first thirty days. Your loved ones who have passed would want you to focus on your life and not be overly enmeshed by grief that prevents you from continuing to live life to the full in the future. When waves of grief come just let it carry you away and cry or shout aloud if needed. Feeling angry is normal as well, **both at** God and sometimes even at the person for dying. Eventually the waves of intense grief will come less often. I still see/experience places and things that will remind me of a departed friend or loved one years after their passing. The wave of grief may still come at those times. It is the price of living a life filled with good connections to others. There is no set time period for grief. For some the worst is over within the first year. For others it may take years. There will always be an empty place in your heart that your departed once occupied. Be comforted knowing that dealing with the grief does get easier with time.

Chapter Ten - Adding Holiness To Our World Through Actions And Words

One night, not long after my ordination, I awoke with an urgent need to write down my thoughts. This following insight is what I wrote.

One of our jobs is to elevate the mundane things in life and add *kedusha*, holiness, to them. We do this through actions and words aimed at producing holiness. For example a utility candle is just some white wax and string. It can be lit to read a pornographic magazine or it can be lit to welcome Shabbat and the Festivals. The difference lies in our intention and the words of blessing we recite. It transforms the lit candle into a holy act.

Wine is simply fermented grape juice. It can be consumed to become drunk or profane. When the blessing over the wine is recited, in moderation it elevates our spirit and sanctifies God.

Eating food sustains us as it does any animal. Add a blessing of gratitude to God and we turn an animalistic act into an act of holiness.

Sex without marriage fills an instinctive need, similar to animals. Add marriage and it is a fulfillment of God's promise to help us form couples and families. God is included in these acts of pleasure that help bind us closer to each other.

Our lips can utter curses or say words of Praise and kindness. We can heal with our words or inflict wounds. Our soul's intention is what makes the difference. We can turn fabric into an executioner's mask or we can turn it into a prayer shawl.

With explosives we can kill others in an act of terror or we can clear obstructions for a road or bridge or hospital to bring people together or heal them.

We can use our bodies to steal, to kill or to harm others without justification. Or we can use them to serve God and others, to be God's partner. What we do and what we say will either help complete our world or help destroy it. It is entirely up to us. Let us choose wisely.

Chapter 11 - There Are No Saints In Judaism – We All Have Our Flaws

In Judaism, we recognize that all people are human, with good qualities as well as frailties and flaws. It was said that when the ancient sage Rabbi Susya was dying, he was sad upon reviewing his life. His students asked him why he was sad as he had led an exemplary life. He told them, *'God will not ask me why weren't you like Moses or like Abraham? I fear that God will ask me, Why weren't you like Susya?'*

We are all judged by our innate potential and how close we come to achieving that potential in our lifetime. In the story of the binding of Isaac, where Abraham seemingly is ready to sacrifice his beloved youngest son per God's commandment, his name is doubled. When the Angel of God orders him not to harm his son, it says 'Abraham, Abraham!' Why the doubling? Rabbi Label Lam compared it to looking at the beautiful photos of flowers on a seed packet. How often does what we grow look like the packet? At that moment Abraham reached his full potential for following God. What God knew he could be, matched with what he actually was.

But I ask, did Abraham completely pass the test? We know that he argued with God to save the wicked residents of Sodom and Gomorrah. He negotiated with God to spare the cities if ten righteous people could be found. A Jewish *minyan*, a quorum for a complete prayer service, consists of 10 Jewish adults based on that negotiation. (10 Jewish men per Orthodox Judaism)

Although God destroyed those cities, it was credited to Abraham's merit that he cared enough to argue for the residents. Indeed, we credit Abraham with being the very first Jew but not his ancestor Noah. Noah was a righteous man, *in his generation*, but in the century of work building the Ark, he did not recruit one passenger outside of his family. Noah did not try to argue with God not to destroy all life on land. It is the empathetic human difference between Noah and Abraham that distinguishes them. Abraham was called God's friend in the Torah. His concern for others made him beloved by God.

Yet when he is commanded to bring Isaac to the place God would show him and offer him there as a burnt offering, he is silent. The Rabbis were so uncomfortable with his silence that they imagined an exchange where Abraham responds to God's words in the text like this:

God: Take your son.

Abraham: I have two sons.

God: Your unique son.

Abraham: Each of my sons is unique in their own way,

God: Whom you love.

Abraham: I love both Ishmael and Isaac.

God: Isaac.

Isaac, who was no youngster, anywhere from 13 years old to 40 by some traditions, could have easily fought and run away from his aged father had he chosen to do so. He did not fight or resist as his trust in his father was absolute. They walked together for days to get to the site, where tradition says centuries later the Temple in Jerusalem would be built. Isaac agrees to lie atop the wood to be sacrificed. Abraham is ready to carry out the commandment. I believe the text gives us a hint that he did not pass the test with flying colors.

Before the near sacrifice, God always spoke or appeared directly to Abraham. After he was ready to bring down the knife to slay Isaac, God only speaks to Abraham through an angel, but never directly again. This would seem to be a lower level of communication using the intermediary angel.

The text also says that Abraham will be blessed 'because you did not withhold your son, your unique son, Isaac from Me.' What is missing from the original commandment to sacrifice

Isaac? '***whom you love***.' The deletion of the word '*love*' is very significant. Perhaps he should have loved his son more and argued on his behalf.

The very next reading in the Torah talks about Sarah's death. There is a Rabbinic *midrash*, a teaching story, that relates the two incidents. Isaac did not go home with his father. It appears from the text that he spent time near where Ishmael settled. When Abraham and the servants returned without Isaac, the *midrash* says Sarah died of shock believing Abraham had slain their son, before she could learn the truth. Odds are that Sarah did not know Abraham's plans when he left with Isaac, as I suspect she would have had some harsh words on the topic. As a family man, Abraham was deeply flawed. Tension between Sarah and Hagar caused Hagar and Ishmael to be banished from his camp. It can be inferred from the fact that Isaac did not return home with him that his relationship with Isaac may have been strained by the near sacrifice. The death of Sarah completes the tragedy. Abraham was a good person, a true follower of God, but like all of us he had his flaws.

Moses, who by Jewish tradition had the closest relationship with God of any human, was denied entry to the Promised Land because he struck a rock in anger to bring forth water instead of speaking to it as God commanded. Speaking to a rock and having it bring forth water would be a clear miracle attributable to God. Hitting the rock to get water would make it look like Moses' actions brought the water. After a lifetime of sacrifice and service, this one act in anger deprived him of the desired end to his journey. He was held to an unusually high standard because his knowledge of God was so intimate.

King David sinned by sending Uriah the Hittite to be killed so he could marry his soon to be widow Bathsheba. Solomon strayed from God by having hundreds of wives, each had his failings and frailties.

This should give each of us hope. God knows we have our flaws and is forgiving. We simply need to be the best people we can be despite our flaws.

The Torah never gives us a commandment that we cannot fulfill. For example we are commanded to love God, and to love our neighbor as we love ourselves. When we think of all of the blessings in our lives loving God is only logical. We can understand loving others as we love ourselves – if only we could do so with a full heart!

Yet in the Fifth of the Ten Commandments we are told to Honor/Respect our fathers and mothers. Why aren't we commanded to love them? A young girl in my religious school class was troubled by the fact that her parents had divorced and her father later married a woman the girl wasn't very comfortable around. She asked me with great concern if she had to love her stepmother?

I said that if she eventually grew to love her, that would be wonderful. The only thing God asked of her was to treat her stepmother with respect and dignity as by so doing she would also be honoring her father. God doesn't command love for parents or step-parents who may not deserve it.

Some people have abusive and horrible childhoods. The 5th Commandment only tells us as adults to make sure our parents have a roof over their heads, food to eat, and basic needs met. We owe our lives to them for their role in creating or raising us, but love has to be something earned in a relationship. We are never commanded to do the impossible.

While there aren't any perfect people, there are saintly people in this world. A kabbalistic tradition says that for the sake of 36 righteous people hidden throughout the world at any time, God allows our world to continue to survive. The 36 can be from any culture, race, religion or background. They may not be recognized by others, but God sees their actions. I believe I knew just that sort of person.

In college I loved astronomy. I took many courses and even designed and built my own telescope. Partly it was because I had a fantastic teacher, Dr. Ed Ortell of El Camino College in Torrance, CA. We became friends and over the years I visited his family home in Mouse Hollow, Iowa and helped lay out an observatory on nearby Leisure Lake. Dr. Ortell is able to tell a story in a captivating way and could bring complex concepts forward in such a way as to make them understandable. He was a WW2 bomber navigator and he had friends on every continent. I remember one year he disappeared for a few months. He simply drove as far south from California as he could and hopped a boat to Antarctica. I received a videotape of him playing with the penguins. He is an amazing person who can relate to everyone he meets.

His wife, June Sagers Ortell, of blessed memory, was a person whom I believe was one of the 36 hidden righteous individuals. A lovely and kind woman, I never heard her speak a harsh or negative word. Her love and concern for others was amazing and inspiring. I remember one visit to the small and immaculate country church she attended in Mouse Hollow, Iowa. Its gleaming white paint was surrounded by a well maintained churchyard where members of the congregation dating back to the civil war were laid to rest. I saw many Sagers on the tombstones but was surprised only to see a few Ortells, although both families had been there for generations. I asked Dr. Ortell about it and he told me *'We Ortells never die'* June smiled and told me that *'they used to bury the horse thieves in the middle of the road'*.

June Ortell loved to read the Bible, particularly the Psalms each day. She developed eye issues that started to rob her of her eyesight. Even as it got worse and worse, I never heard her complain about going blind or express any anger towards God for taking her eyesight. Her one regret was when her eyesight reached the point that she could no longer read the Psalms. She tried an audio version but it just wasn't the same as seeing the words and contemplating their meaning.

I went to see a Muslim man who ran a local Sir Speedy print shop in Torrance. I explained Mrs. Ortell's situation and asked him how large he could blow up the English text of the Psalms. After working on it for awhile he made the letters as large as the biggest letter on an eye-chart. He did the project exactly at his cost. We presented the humongous flip chart style Book of Psalms to Mrs. Ortell who cried with joy when she found that she could still read the beloved words. I believe God smiled when a Muslim and Jew worked together to bring joy to a religious and righteous Christian woman. When Mrs. Ortell passed away, our world became a little bit darker for her passing.

One of my congregants is the Polin family that drives from Laguna Niguel to Torrance to attend Matzo Ball Minyan services. Lew and Gloria have an adult son Howard, who is a true *Tzaddik*, a righteous soul. Born with some learning challenges, the doctors were negative about Howard's ability to live a full life. Howard and God showed them! He is a dearly beloved worker at his local grocery store who has been the subject of story about his life in the newspaper. He lives independently, does beautiful needlepoint work, and loves attending Saturday services. The huge smile and joy it gives Howard to carry the Torah scroll and recite the blessings truly lifts my heart and spirit. His work with the Jeremiah Society of Orange County, CA helps others to live their lives to the full. Thank God for sending us such righteous and good people!

CHAPTER TWELVE - CONVERSATIONS WITH FATHER LUKE DYJAK

One of the fascinating people I had the privilege of knowing, was the late Father Luke Dyjak, of blessed memory. Father Luke was a Franciscan priest who had been a missionary sent to Japan, Turkey and numerous other countries starting in the 1940's. He was a scholar with an intimate knowledge of Hebrew and Aramaic. He had a warm smile and a keen mind. I met Father Luke while accompanying my parents to visit their friend Helen's mother who lived at the Little Sisters of The Poor Jeanne Jugan residence in San Pedro. The Sisters run a beautiful and spotless facility with lots of activities, barbeques and amazing ocean views. Father Luke was a retired priest in failing health who lived there.

When I entered the main building I heard '*Shalom Aleichem Rabbi,*' 'Peace be unto you.' I turned and saw Father Luke dressed in black with a roman collar. '*Aleichem Shalom, Father*' I replied. We became good friends and I looked forward to visiting and studying with him each week. I learned that Father Luke used to live and work in New York and his close friend was an orthodox rabbi. They would study and discuss ancient sacred texts together. They were so close that when his friend the Rabbi suffered a fatal heart attack, his final words were a request that his personal Hebrew English Bible be sent to Father Luke.

I asked Father Luke if he could explain the concept of the Trinity to me. I was at a loss to reconcile it with the Torah's statement that God is One which is a foundation of Jewish belief. It is an aspect of Catholicism I simply couldn't comprehend. Father Luke gave me an explanation that I could understand and would like to share with you. He asked me 'If I give you some ice cubes, what are you holding on a molecular level?' I said 'H_2O'. He said 'If I hand you a glass of water what are you holding in the glass?' Again I replied 'H_2O'. Finally he asked, 'If you boil the water and ice cubes to rising steam, what is the molecular structure of the steam?' Again, I replied 'H_2O'. He said 'That is what the Trinity is about. Just as ice, water and steam look and feel like very different things they are really different ways of experiencing the exact same molecular structure. When Catholics talk about the Father, Son and Holy Spirit, they are just different ways of relating to the One God.'

This I could understand. In Judaism we have many names for God. We pray to 'our Father,' 'My Lord,' 'God Almighty,' 'Our King' and 'The Rock.' Some Hebrew forms of God's name we don't pray to, such as the very formal form of His name used when describing the Flood in the time of Noah, or the God of strict justice that destroyed Sodom and Gomorrah. Just as I am known as a father to my kids, a husband to my wife, an attorney to my legal co-workers, a Rabbi to my congregants, and a son to my parents, all describe different relationships I have with others while I am the same person at all times.

The Hindus will say that they worship many Gods, but they will also say that they only worship one God. They believe it is too hard to relate to Brahma, the name for all encompassing God whose Spirit fills the universe. They relate to Krishna, Shiva, Rama and other personality traits of the One God. There is unity among the world's faiths in the manner of diversity of names with which we pray to God.

I once asked Father Luke if he had ever had the opportunity to become a bishop in the church given his decades of service. He smiled and asked me if I know what the Hebrew word *'Betulah'* means? I said 'virgin.' He then asked me what a *'na-ah-rah'* is? I answered 'a young woman.' He told me he sent a letter to the Vatican in the 1940's pointing out the difference in meaning and suggesting that perhaps Rome should consider the theological impact the different words would have on the faith. That pretty much ended his promotional opportunities. He was a kind and caring man who had a good effect on the world.

When Father Luke passed away in 1998 I was very honored to be invited to recite the Aramaic Mourner's Kaddish for him at his funeral Mass. I mourned his loss and still miss my friend.

Chapter 13 - A Word About Translations versus Original Texts

Have you ever wondered why there is such a proliferation of translations of Bible texts? The Jewish Publication Society has an excellent English translation of the Hebrew Jewish Bible. Christians have the NIV, the King James and various editions. Why the need for so many? From a Jewish perspective, we learn Hebrew to study the text as originally written and sometimes there are numerous ways to interpret a single word.

A Torah scroll, consists of the Hebrew books of Genesis, Exodus, Leviticus, Numbers and Deuteronomy. It takes a specially trained *Sofer*, a scribe, about a year to hand write a Torah scroll. The parchment is made from the skin of a *kosher*, ritually pure, animal. The Hebrew calligraphy is done with great care using a bird feather quill pen and hand made ink. There are no punctuation marks or vowels added, just column after column of capital letters. Torah scrolls can last for many generations and are the most treasured and revered ritual objects used in Judaism. New scrolls can cost $50,000 or more.

Because there are no punctuation marks there can be some question as to how to read a word in the text. While there are traditions about the meaning and pronunciation of the words, the Hebrew can contain many levels of meaning.

For example, virtually every English Bible in the world opens with 'In the beginning God created the heavens and the earth.' The first Hebrew word, *'B'raysheet'* is translated as 'in the beginning' by reading it as follows 'B' (meaning 'In') *RaySheet* meaning 'Beginning.' The word can also be broken up as follows: *'Bah-Rah Shayt'* Aramaic meaning 'He Created for Six' which is also consistent with the story. Or it could be broken up as *'B'Rosh-Yaht'* (meaning 'In the Head (of Time) Only God existed.'

Every one of these translations has a valid meaning. Sadly, when we translate the text, the English limits us to the one most common translation. Commentary may talk about other meanings but to explore it all would make the book unwieldy as all of these meanings are for simply the first word! It is not easy to learn an ancient language such as Hebrew or Aramaic but it does bring the text fully to life to study it in the original. There is a poetry and drama to the words that is somewhat lacking in translation. The language of the Psalms and Song of Songs has an elegance and poetry that is distinctive. When we read the story of Esau trading his spiritual birthright for a bowl of lentil soup (Genesis 25:29-34) the Hebrew text is very abrupt. 'He Ate, He drank, He got up and He left.' The words give us some insight into Esau's abrupt personality.

My custom is not to chant the Torah reading at services, but to read it out loud and discuss these sorts of things as we come upon them. One year I was discouraged because no new insight was coming to me for the first chapter of Genesis. I called Rabbi Gelberman in New York for advice. He asked me to say the first sentence in Hebrew. 'B'raysheet Bara Elohim Et HaShamayim v'et Ha-Aretz. In the beginning God created the heavens and the earth.' He asked me to translate 'Et' – spelled Aleph Taf in Hebrew, the first and last letters of the alphabet. I said it is a grammatical tool to point to the subject of a sentence and has no translation. Rabbi Gelberman said 'In the beginning, God created A-Z, everything in the heavens and the earth.' Such an insight! The text is the same each year. We are different though, changed by our life experiences. Are any of us the same people we were a year ago or five years ago? There is always something new to glean from the sacred words, so study them and turn them over and over like a fine gemstone.

Chapter 14 - The Story Of How We Obtained A Very Old Torah Scroll – The Native American Casino Miracle

At Congregation Beth Torah in Torrance we had a very special Torah scroll that was donated to the congregation by one of our Board members, Mr. Michael Kraus. Mike knew that one of our older scrolls was very worn and the cost to fix it was many thousands of dollars. He found a scroll that was removed from its rollers for sale on eBay. The seller was in Israel and had good feedback from buyers. Mike placed a bid. A few days later while vacationing at the Pechanga Indian Casino Resort in Temecula, California, Mike's iPhone dinged and told him he had won the scroll for $1,150. He paid for it immediately using PayPal. He then dropped a nickel in a slot machine, pulled the handle and won $5,000.00. When the scroll arrived in 2008 it needed some minor repairs and had to be fitted onto rollers for use. The cost? $5,000! His slot winnings gave us a beautiful and huge Torah scroll.

In Passover 2009 we used the scroll for the first time. The writing was clear and beautiful. The text had some special calligraphy ornamentation to certain letters which were unusual.

When we reached the Book of Numbers we found two purple oval stamp marks on the back of the scroll. They said 'Department De La Muerte.' I photographed the marks and asked local experts if they knew what it meant. They were unaware of the meaning. Eventually I was referred to an expert in the Czech Republic and emailed the photos to her. Amazingly, the marks indicated that the scroll was seized during the French Revolution's Reign of Terror. Further research showed the scroll was written by a Hasidic scribe, who used special ornamentation on certain letters as part of a very old Kabbalistic tradition. The metallic content of the ink indicated it was an already old scroll during the days of French Revolution, possibly from the late 17th Century or very early 18th Century.

The Torah scroll had been seized from the congregation in Nancy, France around July 28, 1794. During that period synagogues and churches were being raided for valuables. Many years later the Emperor Napolean Bonaparte returned these items to their rightful owners.

Our belief is that during the Holocaust, a Rabbi or Congregant took the parchment off the wooden rollers and hid it. It was probably brought to Israel after the war by a survivor. When that person passed away the estate sold it to the seller who eventually listed it on eBay. The scroll has an almost velvety feel to the parchment from being rolled and re-rolled over the centuries. Imagine how many people touched the scroll, studied from it and taught others from it over the centuries? It is the oldest Torah scroll I have ever used in a service and all of our 13 year old and adult Bar and Bat Mitzvah students choose to read from this scroll, although it is very large and heavy. What a journey and life it has had and continues to have.

Chapter 15 - What is the Purpose and Meaning of Life?

My uncle, Dr. Louis Lunsky, M.D., of blessed memory, used to tell the story of elderly Mrs. Cohen of Brooklyn. A widow, she lived a quiet life. One time she told her Rabbi that she was about to travel to Mongolia to meet the High Lama. The Rabbi was shocked!

'Mrs. Cohen, that is a long and arduous journey! In order to get to Mongolia you will have to take a plane around the world, followed by a long train ride. You will then have to ride a Yak to the high mountain abbey where he holds court. If you have a question about the meaning of life I assure you the answer can be found in the Torah without going to such lengths!'

She thanked the Rabbi but was adamant. She flew 17 hours to get to China. Then she rode for three days on a train to Mongolia. She mounted a yak for the two day journey to the high mountain pass where the High Lama's abbey stood in the snowy, howling wind.

A guard asked her why she had come? She said 'to see the High Lama.' The guard assured her that the High Lama was too busy to see people unannounced. She said 'I will wait.'

After waiting for three days the High Lama agreed to an audience with Mrs. Cohen. The great bronze doors emblazoned with dragons swung open and she stepped into the High Lama's chamber. Candles were lit and flickering and incense burned continually. The High Lama was seated on a raised dais resplendent in his flowing orange robes.

Mrs. Cohen looked at him and said 'Sheldon, it is time to come home.'

The meaning and purpose of life has been discussed since people could first communicate with each other. I want to share with you my belief about why you were born at the particular time and place of your birth, as ordered by God. I completely accept that God chooses the date of our birth and ultimately the date of our passing from the world. Whether we live only a few hours or 120 years as granted to Moses, there is a definite purpose to it all. My beloved teacher, Rabbi Joseph H. Gelberman, of blessed memory, used to say that since God completed creating the world, He has chosen not to do things alone.

We are God's partners, here to carry out His Will, even though we may not consciously know that is what we are doing. I want you to reflect on your life. Think of those times when someone really changed your life by saying the right thing or by doing something for you.

There was a story on a suicide and bullying prevention website called 'Jared's Story' many years ago that I shared with my congregation one Yom Kippur day. I believe it was also included in the original 'CHICKEN SOUP FOR THE SOUL' book in 1994.

To paraphrase it, a valedictorian speaker at a high school stunned the graduates and families in attendance. He gave a tribute to his best friend and thanked him for saving his life. His friend was stunned, not believing he had done anything of the sort. When they were freshmen the boy who would become valedictorian was carrying a large load of textbooks in his hands one Friday after school. A bully shoved the boy and knocked his books to the ground while laughing at him. Another young man rushed over and helped pick up all of the books. They started talking and became friends. Four years later they were graduating. The speaker, again, to paraphrase, said *'You never asked me why I was carrying home all of my books that day. You see, the bullying had worn me down such that I was going home to kill myself. I didn't want my mother to have to come to school and empty out my locker, so I did it myself. When that bully knocked the books down it reinforced to me that life is not worth living. Because of your kindness and friendship I held off on suicide. Truly I owe you my life.'*

A simple action or kind word may save a life and we may never know it. This is a two edged sword however. A harsh word or unkind act may have devastating consequences. It is up to us to decide the impact of our deeds and words.

One Shabbat morning my Congregation had two visitors, an attorney named Paul and his wife from Century City. Paul's mother had just died and the cemetery referred them to me to officiate on Sunday at the funeral as his own Rabbi was not available.

By Jewish tradition we bury very quickly, usually within one to two days if at all possible. I had asked if they could attend Saturday morning services and I would sit with them afterwards to learn about his mother's life and create a personalized ceremony and eulogy that night.

It was the custom in my congregation that any visitors would be asked to be involved in the service and to be made to feel a part of the congregation. We called the couple up for Torah blessing honors.

The wife was quite nervous as she had never done the blessings before. We had a large transliteration of the words on the reader's table and she did very well. When I confirmed that it was her first time being called to the Torah we said the *Shehechiyanu* prayer thanking God for allowing us to experience this joyous moment.

My good friend, Rabbi Ken Giss, came forward and presented her with a ballpoint pen as we pronounced this to be her Bat Mitzvah day. There is an old custom of giving a fountain pen to a Bar or Bat Mitzvah student, when they are first called to the Torah. From that moment onward they are morally responsible for their own decisions and the pen symbolizes writing their own future.

I met with them afterwards and officiated at the funeral the next day. They lived far away from my synagogue and I did not see them again for a number of years.

Then Paul called me up and informed me that his wife had

just passed away after a battle with cancer. I was greatly saddened to hear this as she was still a young woman and I remembered her to be a very nice person. I said I would be honored to officiate but was curious why he chose me instead of his own local Rabbi?

What he said floored me. *'My wife was born Jewish but had no involvement in the religion. She might accompany me to a service but had not studied about Judaism. After you pronounced her to be a Bat Mitzvah, she told me that she felt obligated to learn a little bit about Judaism. She read a Jewish book and soon we lit Friday night Shabbat candles together at home. That December, for the first time, we lit the Hanukkah menorah together with our family and said the blessings. She started taking some adult education classes at our synagogue and became more involved. When the cancer was diagnosed her faith helped her endure the treatments. When we knew the cancer was terminal she was calm about her impending death. The last words she spoke were the Shma prayer, "Hear O' Israel, the Lord is our God, the Lord is One." Your congregation celebrating her Bat Mitzvah enriched our lives and let her die at peace with God. That is why I want you to officiate at her funeral."*

I barely remembered the spontaneous bat mitzvah as we have done it at other times for other visitors. I could never have imagined that such a small thing I didn't think twice about, had such a profound impact on her life and death.

Every one of us impacts those around us. What we may not even think twice about, may be the most important thing in the world to another person. Have you ever thought to yourself, I should call so and so and see how they are doing? Or maybe I should bring some food to a neighbor who just suffered a loss. Maybe you went to visit someone in the hospital. I tell you now that those interior prompts are God telling you where you are needed. God speaks to us constantly, but do we listen?

Sometimes the messages are quite direct. I remember having lunch at a Chinese restaurant with my parents in 1988. I was 23 years old. After the Kung Pao Beef came the sliced sweet oranges and fortune cookies. I told my mother that I was at a crossroads. I could either pursue my love of Astronomy by studying for an advanced degree in the field or I could apply to law school.

Only 1% of Astronomy doctorates ever get to work directly in the field. Law school would be similar to my yeshiva studies, but not knowing any lawyers, I did not know if it was the right pursuit for me. I cracked open my fortune cookie and the strip of paper said *'You would make a good lawyer.'* That decided me.

I took the LSAT test and was accepted soon after to Whittier College School of Law. Three years later I received my Juris Doctor degree and passed the California Bar Exam on the first try. 21 years later I am still enjoying the practice of law. I framed that fortune cookie strip and kept it as a reminder to be open to messages.

If there are times when you are trying very hard to go in a certain direction, but time after time you are making no headway at all, perhaps it is also a message to consider another pathway.

Perhaps we need to be born in a certain time and place so that our children or grandchildren will accomplish something amazing. Every one of us has a purpose and a reason for living.

People ask me what do I pray for as a Rabbi? Besides the prayers for recovery and good health for others and my loved ones, I thank God each day for making my wife and kids and I a family.

Perhaps most importantly, I ask God privately each morning to show me how to be useful that day. If there is someone I am supposed to help or to interact with, please let me know when that moment arrives.

In a way we are each like an employee of a large corporation that is sent out to do the work of the corporation. While you are on company business your travel and food expenses will often be covered. If you open yourself up to being God's representative, God will give you whatever you need to do the job. Will the road be easy? Probably not. Will we have pain and difficulty in life? Yes, it is the cost of being born and living. Perhaps most importantly, our lives will have great meaning and impact others. When we eventually pass away a good reputation endures forever.

Chapter 16 - Are All Religious Paths Equally Valid?

I strongly believe that God revealed part of his total message to mankind in a myriad of ways. Jewish tradition tells us that when God gave us the Ten Commandments at Mount Sinai after leaving Egypt, no two persons heard it the same way. Some heard the words as a quiet whisper in silence. Others heard a booming voice that seemed earth shattering. Whatever language a person spoke was the language in which they heard the Words spoken. It is said that all 10 were given at the same instant so that each is equally important. It was the one time the human mind could comprehend and remember the ten statements spoken at once.

Similarly the world's great faiths communicate very similar ideals to humankind. Love one another, be kind to strangers, care for the widow and the orphan and the poor. Don't steal, don't murder, be a good person. Any religion that has this positive message is valid and acceptable to God.

If you are born into a faith that has no resonance at all for you after you have explored and studied it, it is far better to find another faith that lets you connect to God rather than to live a life devoid of faith or spirituality.

So called religions such as Satanism, Santa Muerte, Voodoo, Santeria and other practices that revere and call upon the darkness are *not* valid. Sacrificing animals or placing curses to harm others does not help bring peace or light into this world.

Extremists of any valid faith who twist the word of God to justify terrorism and senseless hatred and violence do not serve God and should be condemned by the faithful worldwide. Religion should bring us closer to mankind as well as to God. I love participating in interfaith events where we share our ways of worshipping and meditating together.

Please note that I am **not** calling for one world religion or for a blending of different faith traditions into a conglomerated religion. Instead I pray that we will each see the beauty and uniqueness of other faiths and be not just tolerant, but *loving*, to each other.

About half of my congregation consisted of interfaith couples. The question would arise about how to handle the Christmas/Chanukah and Easter/Passover holidays, particularly when young children are in the family.

My answer is to celebrate each holiday in its own tradition, but don't jumble them up. For example when Chanukah and Christmas overlap, have one table set with the menorah and Jewish holiday decorations. If a Christmas tree is used, have it and its ornaments separate from the Chanukah display. No Chanukah bushes! No menorah ornaments on the tree. Explain to the children that Mommy and Daddy or each set of grandparents celebrates a different holiday. Teach them about the true story and meaning of each holiday. Explain that just as we can help our friends celebrate their birthdays even though it isn't our party, we can help each side of the family to celebrate their holidays.

The same goes for Easter and Passover. If they coincide make the Seder dinner distinct from the Easter celebration. I would point out that each holiday comes in the Spring to celebrate redemption and new life. For the Jews Passover meant an end to slavery and the start of a new life of freedom and dedication to God. Easter tells the story of sacrifice done for the redemption of humanity, a tremendous gift of love.

Kids will get it. As long as they are taught to be respectful of all, they will feel comfortable in any gathering.

Chapter 17 - My Ideal House Of God

I know from speaking with a Muslim Imam, Ashraf Carrim, and other clergy, that we all have similar issues for which we try to assist congregants. Difficulty in marriages or relationships, concern for children, health challenges, dealing with grief and loss, financial stress, all humans have similar basic problems. I am guessing that most of us could switch places with other clergy and be dealing with the same sort of problems. Imagine going to one spiritual place where you could observe the various forms of worship and the way in which different religions and cultures meet these challenges!

If my dream were to come true, I would love to see a true House of God built. In one building, congregations of Jews, Christians, Muslims, Hindus, Baha'i, Buddhists and others would have separate rooms/halls dedicated to their form of worship. The clergy would each be people who cherish interfaith work and have a true love of God in all the forms God is worshipped. Attendees could go from hall to hall to celebrate or witness the services, discussions and celebrations of each faith.

In a large central hall or auditorium interfaith panel discussions and activities would take place. Group meals could be shared with respect for the dietary traditions of each faith. All could stand together as a community of faith in times of sorrow or joy. Each religion would be distinct and separate and yet accessible to all.

A similar idea for the Monotheistic faiths of Judaism, Christianity and Islam under one roof is being built in Germany. My friend Imam Ashraf Carrim and his wife Athia talked about this at an interfaith Ramadan Iftar (break the fast evening meal) at their mosque in Carson, California, called the International Institute of Tolerance. The German house of worship for the three faiths is called the House of One and I wish them great success. My congregation and the Imam's congregation have done a number of interfaith programs together over the years. I believe the mutual respect and understanding we have for each other is worth more than all of the politicians' speeches put together.

I would love to see an even more inclusive building built here in Southern California where we will house as many of the great world faiths under one roof as possible. I would hope that people of faith could join together to make this a reality one day, rather than simply having interfaith events at different houses of worship. Imagine a choir that praises God together in various languages and music! God willing, that day will come to be.

CHAPTER 18 - INCLUDING ANIMALS IN OUR SPIRITUAL LIVES

I love to tell a story about the first time Sheryl and I took our kids to a local pumpkin patch at the Del Amo Mall in Torrance in late October 2008. The ground was covered in straw and goats and sheep walked among the people. They also had Llamas, a pig and some horses. Esther and James were having a great time feeding and petting the different creatures who approached them without fear.

With me, it was a different story. The pig and the horse came to me to be pet and fed but the sheep and goats stayed away. It occurred to me that for many centuries bearded Jews used goats and sheep for sacrificial offerings.

In ancient times lambs would be washed in the Kidron stream below Jerusalem in preparation for the Passover sacrifices. There were so many lambs that it looked as if the valley was full of snow to a viewer on the Temple Mount. Perhaps there is a species memory warning *kosher* (ritually and dietary pure) animals to keep their distance from bearded rabbis, even though the sacrifices stopped in 70 A.D. after the Second Temple fell to Rome. The pigs and horses who were never used for such purposes by Jews came up to me cheerfully.

I know that animals have souls and can show compassion, love and concern for others, even those of different species. As a law school student, to save expenses, my parents graciously allowed me to live at home. I had a beloved dog, a golden brown and white basset hound named Watson. I had raised him from a puppy and he had a great personality and the most soulful eyes I have ever seen.

One day a petite silver tabby female feral cat came to my parent's backyard and was fascinated by Watson's 12" dangling ears, long body and deep "woof." She started hanging around the backyard following Watson everywhere. My Mom felt sorry for the skinny cat and started putting out food and water in the backyard for her. Eventually she would rub up against the dog and engage him in play.

The day came when the cat followed Watson through the pet door into the house. She loved the dog and was not afraid of people, but did not want to be touched or pet by people. Treating her with flea medicine was an ordeal as she had to be wrapped in a towel to prevent her from shredding us. She would give a warning meow, which if ignored would be followed up with a swift strike of her paw, claws extended. My Mom called the cat Tiki.

Tiki learned that Watson, who usually tried to ignore her, would mistake her purring for growling. Watson would then softly growl back at her. Tiki learned not to purr at Watson but contented herself with grooming him and taking naps between his huge paws and under his ears. After a few months of this, but still not able to touch Tiki, I grew concerned that the cat might badly scratch my parents, both of whom had fragile skin and bled easily. While talking with my folks about this, Tiki left the room. She went into our neighbor's yard where he had tall palm trees. Within minutes she returned and threw down the biggest dead rat I have ever seen with a huge body and tail that was bigger than Tiki herself.

My Mom decided on the spot that she could stay since she was willing to wipe out any rodents near the house. Years later my wife would say maybe she threw it down as a warning to me not to try and evict her! With time she would climb into my Mom's lap and allow herself to be petted. She started purring and showing affection back. She warmed up to me as well and became an accepted part of the family.

In 2002 Watson suddenly lost weight and cried out when he was touched. He was diagnosed with end stage cancer at only 9 years old.

Euthanizing him was one of the most heartbreaking decisions I would ever have to make but I couldn't bear to see him in pain with no hope of recovery. I asked for his remains to be cremated. Tiki was going crazy for several days calling for Watson and searching the house and yard for him. We could not console her. After a few days I brought the container with

Watson's ashes into the house. Tiki went up to the container, sniffed it and gave a very mournful meow. She curled up next to it and took a nap. When she arose later she stopped looking for Watson for good. Somehow she understood that her good friend was dead.

Five years later my Mom was in her bed on hospice care for the breast cancer. Tiki never left her side. In the last few days, when my Mom was in a comatose state, Tiki stopped eating and only left the bed to go to the bathroom and then would immediately return. She did not attack the nurses who gave Mom shots and fluids. If anyone else tried to touch my mother Tiki would give them a stern warning with her claws out. After my mother's death Tiki finally left her side and started eating and drinking water again. I was so grateful that our friend Dr. Mona Bloom was willing to adopt Tiki as we were going to Vietnam in a few days and did not want to leave her in our home, with our cats that she didn't know. It was unthinkable to leave her in my Mom's empty house. Mona gave her a good life, which she richly deserved. I am sure her soul and Watson's are with my Mom in God's blazing light of joy.

Many years earlier I had a parrot, a Mexican Red-Headed Amazon, which I talked out of a tree in Orange County one fourth of July in the late 1970's. We posted flyers but nobody claimed him and the Animal Shelter and Police did not receive any calls about a lost parrot. I named him 'Tookie' – which is Hebrew for 'parrot.'

As a matter of trivia it is thought that Jewish sailors on Christopher Columbus' ships, fleeing Spain in the expulsion of the Jews of 1492, first saw wild turkeys in America and thought their colorful tail feathers meant they were a species of parrot unknown in Spain. They called them Tookies as well, and the word transformed into 'Turkey' in English.

My bird Tookie was quite the character. He loved sitting on my shoulder and would eat any pencils I held and shred anything

I was trying to read. He hated being pet but tolerated it while growling at me. He used to crack open red hot dried chili peppers and lick the seeds from them like they were candy. He would then lean over and kiss my lip, setting it on fire. How he would laugh as I rushed to get a drink to extinguish the burn!

On Shabbat I would give Tookie a thimble of sweet wine while we made the blessings. He would take a sip, sing happily and then take a snooze. He could speak with both a New York and a Californian accent. My parents had a large dog named Rex, and he would call the dog in my parent's voices and then laugh at it when Rex came into the room thinking my parents or I had called him.

One day I rescued an injured parakeet from a neighbor's cat. We couldn't locate the owner and we cared for the parakeet. One day Tookie was standing on top of the parakeet cage to get a look at the much smaller bird. The parakeet started biting Tookie's feet. Tookie was clearly upset but didn't say a word in front of the parakeet. I carried him into the kitchen where he was out of sight of the parakeet. He then threw a screaming wall-eyed fit. He knocked things off of shelves with his wings, kicked things to the ground and shredded anything he could get his beak around. He simply had too much dignity to show his anger in front of the smaller bird.

Tookie went with me to Yeshiva University of Los Angeles and stayed in my dorm room with my roommate and I. He learned some Hebrew words and phrases and was well known and liked at the school. One day I was studying in my room and had covered Tookie's cage with an apron to make it darker for him to rest. To my horror he pulled the Apron strings into the cage, twisted them into a noose, shoved his head through it and stepped off of his perch, swinging by the neck. My roommate and I rushed over and rescued him. I vowed to use only a towel in the future for a cage cover but nothing with strings.

The Rosh HaYeshiva, Rabbi Shalom Tendler, the head of the school, heard about this and summoned Tookie and I into his office.

The Rabbi was dressed in very traditional Rabbinic garb with a long black coat and full dark beard. He spoke directly to Tookie. 'I have heard you talk and believe you have a good soul. You speak and understand English. I want you to know that things are never so terrible that you should ever try and take your own life. This would be a *shanda*, a scandal, and would devastate many people here.' The bird carefully listened to every word and never again did any action to harm himself.

My wife and I have four cats, two Siamese cats, a Tonkinese cat, and a domestic shorthair rescue cat. Our Tonkinese cat Winston is my baby. He loves to be held on his back and does 'kneady paws' of happiness while Sheryl and I sing to him. We adopted him about nine years ago along with his sister Shadow. The two were very close and always stayed together.

Shadow's health was fragile and she died several years ago. Winston was depressed and inconsolable, refusing to eat and laying still. Our most senior cat, a gorgeous and regal large Seal Point Siamese named Major Tom, stayed at Winston's side for a full week, grooming him and napping with his paws around Winston. When Winston started eating again Major Tom gave him more space.

How many times do we see on the news dogs and cats saving their owner's lives? There is compassion and love in them. I wish more humans had such compassion and love in their dealings with others.

Sheryl and I once had two pet rats, Whiskers and Robin, before we had so many cats. I wasn't sure if I wanted to share our home with rats but knew how Sheryl had loved her pet mouse Mazal, of blessed memory. We went to a Pet store and asked to see two baby rats. The rat we would call Whiskers immediately climbed to my shoulder, burrowed into my beard and gave me a kiss followed by beard grooming. I was sold on them completely. They were like little dogs showing affection and joy at being with people. Unlike hamsters and pet mice, rats like company and love to play with each other and with people. They never bit anyone or acted aggressively. The rats used to live in a huge three level cage. We put special small furniture in the cage for them to sit and play on. It was amusing to watch them move a small sofa together like small movers using their hand like paws until they got it into the right place. As an experiment we tried relocating the sofa but they both moved it back to where they wanted it. They loved their cage so much they really didn't want to leave it for a smaller one while the big one was being cleaned.

My wife and I thought we had a solution. We placed fresh fruit and their favorite treats on a paper towel in the small cage. We opened the doors to each cage and assumed they would go into the small cage to eat their snacks. They just looked at each other for a moment and somehow communicated. Then they simultaneously used their little hands to grasp each edge of the paper towel and pulled it into the big cage without spilling the fruit. Sheryl and I had to laugh. Sheryl has a Master's degree in Library and Information Science and I have a Doctorate in Law. We both had been outsmarted by two rats!

At my synagogue we had a special Animal Appreciation service every year on the Saturday we read the story of Noah's Ark from the Torah scroll each Fall. All pets were welcome to attend. We had a variety of dogs, cats, ferrets, reptiles and even some fish in bowls attend. We read special poetry about pets and said prayers for military, police, rescue, service and therapy animals. We raised funds for local animal charities. We said prayers of healing for sick pets and remembered pets that had passed away. Finally each person was invited to select a Hebrew name for their pet based on their unique personalities, and we blessed the animals and said prayers for those animals in need of rescue.

I was once asked if the souls of our beloved pets live on after their death. I always said I hope so since their souls are some of the kindest and most pure in existence.

An experience at my home makes me **positive** that they go on. I grew up with large dogs as pets. I had no experience with cats before Tiki came into my parent's life. My wife Sheryl was just the opposite. She grew up surrounded by Siamese and Abyssinian cats. She rescued a black and white tuxedo kitten, a domestic shorthair. She named him Fortune, after famed anthropologist Margaret Mead's second husband, Rio Fortune.

Fortune was a great cat who lived a very long life, 17 ½ years. When we were dating, Fortune wasn't too sure if he approved of me, as he could smell basset hound fur on my clothes. That lasted until I cooked some oven baked chicken which he enjoyed. As long as I was useful to him by cooking yummy things it was OK for me to be in his and Sheryl's life.

When we married and moved to Torrance in 2002, Fortune came with us. Watson's death happened a few months before our wedding as had the mouse Mazal's passing. Sheryl has always had a very special relationship with cats. They love to pile on top of her and play with her and snooze on her. Growing up, her father James R. Joiner, of blessed memory, used to joke that he would have to fill the house to the rafters with cats to get one to lay on him as long as Sheryl was there.

Fortune often slept with us at night, usually at the foot of the bed, or on our legs. One night it was quite cold and so we used a crocheted afghan on top of the blankets. It had been hand made by Sheryl's beloved great grandmother, of blessed memory.

I was quite drowsy but I clearly felt the paws of a large, heavy cat circling on my chest before laying down. I assumed Fortune decided to crash out on me and took my hand from under the blanket to pet him. I reached for where I felt the cat but didn't touch anything. This happened twice more. My assumption was that Fortune must have left my chest each time I reached for him, but I never felt him leave, just the paws and weight on my chest. When I really woke up I saw that Fortune was asleep at the foot of the bed on Sheryl's side.

Sheryl then stunned me by asking if I had also felt Delilah, a large Siamese cat she had who had died several years earlier at the ripe old age of 19 ½.

I had never met Delilah. Sheryl told me that Delilah used to like to sleep on the afghan we were using. Occasionally her ghost, for want of a better word, would come to visit Sheryl at night and she would feel the weight of the cat and her paws.

This struck me as amazing because I definitely felt the weight and individual paws on my chest. I asked Sheryl where Delilah used to lay on her and she told me on her chest, which is where I felt this ghost cat. So the answer is yes, animal souls do live on after death. I have never been visited by Delilah again after that night although very occasionally she will visit Sheryl.

Pets have souls and I have no doubt that when we pass away our beloved friends will be waiting for us in God's blazing and joyous light.

Chapter 19 - The Most Challenging Part of Scripture – Judges Chapter 11.

I was once asked what part of the Bible I felt was the most difficult to understand. There are difficult stories throughout all of the books, but the one that personally offends me the most is the story of a Jewish general named Yiftach (Jephthah in English) and his daughter. The story is found in Judges, chapter 11. Yiftach was a social outcast. His mother supposedly was a prostitute and he did not act like of a man of decent character.

Israel at the time was at war with the Ammonites and the war was not going well. Yiftach's neighbors knew he could fight and could strategize military attacks. They asked him to lead them into battle. At first he declined, figuring that they never treated him well and they could jolly well fight their own battles.

God revealed Himself to Yiftach and asked him to lead the troops. Yiftach agreed to do so. He had some serious doubts about their chances in battle and made a vow to God. *"If You deliver the Ammonites into my hands, then whatever comes out of the door of my house to meet me on my safe return from the Ammonites shall be the Lord's and shall be offered by me as a burnt offering"* (Judges 11:29-31) He must have been thinking that a goat or other kosher animal would run up to him, I would assume.

After the battle, his teenage daughter, who is not named in the story, runs out to greet him. He cries out that she has brought grief down on his head and explains his Vow made to God. The daughter asks to go to the mountains for two months with her girlfriends to bewail her youth/virginity and then she will come home to be sacrificed as her father vowed. She comes home and is slaughtered and offered as a burnt offering. It became the custom that all young women in ancient Israel would take four days a year to chant dirges for her. (Judges 11:39-40)

When I first read this story I was absolutely horrified. If God could talk to Yiftach and ask him to lead an army, couldn't God have told him not to do this?

The Torah calls human sacrifice an abomination in several places, so how could Yiftach for a minute imagine that this would be acceptable?

Why don't we know the girl's name as she clearly was devoted to God? Where was her mother and what involvement in this did she have?

Some commentary suggests that she was not in fact killed and burned but was dedicated by her father to God's service, forever remaining a virgin, and perhaps becoming sort of the first Nun. That doesn't coordinate well with the plain language of the Hebrew text which explicitly means an offering totally consumed by fire.

There is an ancient commentary going back several thousand years which says that Yiftach wrote and asked the High Priest to come to Gilead from Jerusalem to relieve him from his vow. The High Priest wrote back that since Yiftach made the ignorant vow, Yiftach should travel to Jerusalem and be absolved at the Temple Mount. Neither side would budge and the girl died.

The only positive thing I can get from this is the lesson that people need to be so careful of what they say or do. Don't count on God stepping in to save the day when we get ourselves into trouble. Furthermore, parents in particular have to let go of their egos to take care of their children. Do whatever you have to in order to avoid harming them. The innocent kids will get hurt when the parents do wrong. I still shudder reading this text.

Chapter 20 - Lessons I Have Learned From Others

I have been very fortunate to know some wonderful people. At Congregation Beth Torah in Torrance I used to keep office hours on Monday evenings. Anyone who wished to speak with me could just drop in. We were renting space in an office building and often I would be the only person there other than those who would come to visit. Every week, like clockwork, congregant Harvey Williams, of blessed memory, would come by to talk, keep me company, and help me get ready for the following Shabbat services. We would roll the Torah scroll to the correct spot in advance. Harvey was a fascinating person. He was African-American, born Jewish, and one of the most deeply faithful Jews I have ever known.

Life was not easy for Harvey. Growing up he faced discrimination both because of his race and his religion. Other Jewish congregations in years past did not treat him or his lovely wife Pat as they should have.

Harvey was always ready to help and participated in Torah discussions with his keen mind. Whenever I would try to thank him for an act of kindness, he smiled and refused. He would point to the sky and say *'Don't thank me, thank the One who sent me.'* That really stuck with me, the sheer humility and loyalty to God contained in that statement. I am making an effort to adopt the statement and use it as my own.

Harvey would attend the funerals of each of our congregants who passed away. He personally would labor by hand to fill in their graves after the funeral, saying that each person deserved to be laid to rest with love from a friend who knew them.

When my Dad died on Thursday November 3, 2005 we had to rush to have him buried before sundown on Friday November 4th. We had a late afternoon funeral service and the sky was growing dark as Shabbat was getting ready to start. Harvey insisted on finishing the task of filling in the grave by hand even though it meant staying on into Shabbat. He actively looked for opportunities to serve God at every opportunity. When cancer claimed his life several years later, his son and our congregation made sure that we lovingly laid every spadeful of earth to complete the burial for him. I will always miss him.

Harry Rotenberg, of blessed memory, was also a fascinating and brilliant man. He was educated in a yeshiva in Poland prior to the Holocaust. His training was brutal with his rabbi making him stand outside in the snow or delivering a whipping for errors in his Hebrew studies. Despite this, he was a gentle and kind man. One Shabbat, on a Saturday morning, I couldn't find my place in the Torah scroll. It seemed as though every sentence said '*Vaydaber Hashem El Moshe Laymor.*' 'And God spoke to Moses saying...' I spent a solid ten minutes trying to find the place I needed without success. Harry, who was well advanced in years, stood up and came to the Torah stand. He was nearly blind but glanced at the scroll, pointed to a spot and said 'here.' He was absolutely correct, finding in an instant the proper spot in the repetitive columns of Hebrew text. He had never forgotten the hard learned lessons from nearly 75 years earlier.

May Massler and Regina Katz were ladies who pushed the envelope on women's roles in the synagogue. My congregation used to be very conservative. Only men would read from the Torah or lead prayers. May and Regina several decades ago both stood firm that women should have equal roles. It caused a split in the congregation with the traditionalists leaving. Because of their bravery, generations of bat mitzvahs, female cantors and leaders became a part of our synagogue history. Jo Kahn, the last President of our Congregation before it merged with another in 2012, carried on the tradition of good stewardship. I had the honor of officiating at her adult Bat Mitzvah as well as those of her grandchildren. These ladies taught me always to be inclusive.

Other founding members, Marshall and Sylvia Saben, Irving

Smuckler, Al & Marilyn Horowitz, all were very advanced in years but made the synagogue a focus of their lives. Whether it was mopping the floor, repairing the ark, wiring the memorial board, organizing events and serving on the Board, they volunteered and got it done. Nancy Benowitz filmed every synagogue event for decades and made photo montages. At our synagogue's 60th Anniversary celebration her photos showed so many familiar faces from years past. Some of the younger parents in the congregation could see their own baby and childhood photos as part of these montages. Nancy and Norm preserved our heritage.

Our students taught me many things as well. Suzanne and Elise Boretz, twins who were very gifted students, took part in the *Locks of Love* campaign donating their long lovely hair to help make wigs for childhood cancer patients. Wendy Magid honored a holocaust child victim during her Bat Mitzvah. There was Alex, a boy who was into goth dress & music. He dressed in black, once getting the metal rings adorning his pants caught on a Torah scroll he was holding during a service. Al Horowitz finally got him loose. My wife, Rebbetzin Sheryl, used to give him advice on his black fingernail polish about how to avoid chips in the finish.

When I was a boy, the first time I said blessings in front of the congregation was on my Bar Mitzvah day at age 13. I remember being quite nervous. My custom is to have my students start to lead prayers by ages 11 and 12. It allows the congregation to get to know them and see the progress they are making. The students are comfortable by the time of their Bar or Bat Mitzvah as they know the prayers and the congregants as well. It is such a pleasure to watch young kids become teenagers and then young adults. The teaching aspect has always been my favorite part of being first a Hebrew school teacher and then later a Rabbi. Teens in particular will ask the hard questions and debate morality and Jewish law. I love to see them struggle with, discuss and come to understand some very challenging life questions.

Chapter 21 - Stories And Lessons I Learned From My Family

The biggest influences on my life were undoubtedly my parents Pearl and Robert Spero and my maternal grandmother Esther Lunsky. They taught me to believe in myself and work hard to pursue my dreams. They knew that persistent hard work will ultimately garner results.

The part of Manhattan where I was ordained, the Lower East Side, has a strong connection to my family. My maternal grandfather, originally from Skidel in Lithuania, had his name changed from Luniansky to Lunsky at Ellis Island. He arrived just before WW1 and returned to Europe to fight in the U.S. Army during the Great War. My paternal great grandfather David, whose last name used to be Shapiro in Odessa, Russia, had his name changed to Spero at Ellis Island.

He fled a 25 year forced conscription into the Czar's army and bought passage for himself and his horse to the United States. My dad told of seeing a very old photo of Great Grandfather David and his horse selling seltzer water and soda from a cart in the Lower East Side. He was quite a character who started each day with a shot of Vodka before getting out of bed. It must have done him some good as he lived to 104, with his wife Sue passing a few hours after him at age 102.

My maternal Grandmother Esther C. Lunsky was born in 1890 and grew up in Worcestor Massachusetts. She was the only girl in a family with 11 sons. She met and married my grandfather Nathan Lunsky prior to World War One after he came to the United States from Lithuania.

My mother, Pearl Ann Spero, was the young sister to my Uncle Lou, both born in the 1920's. During the depression, my mother and her brother Louis Lunsky lived in the back of a tiny, narrow and long store my Grandfather Nathan Lunsky had on Steinway Street in Astoria, (Queens) Long Island. It is hard to imagine four people and a dog living in such a small space. One of my mother's uncles was very handy and he made some room partitions for at least the appearance of some privacy.

The dog was a lovely Spitz dog with gorgeous and thick white fur. My grandmother would wash the dog in Ivory soap and his fur was very full. They adopted the dog for security as he had a horrible disposition and was feared by most everyone in the neighborhood.

The dog adored my grandmother Esther but others had to be very careful. You could bring anything you wanted into the store. The problem was trying to take something out. A paying customer once tried to leave with his purchase and the dog charged him. The customer jumped atop a display case and the dog ripped the heel off of his shoe. In order for my mother and uncle to take their books to school, the dog had to be locked away. They never got robbed however and even the local patrolman would not try to see if the door was locked at night out of fear for what the dog would do him if it opened.

My uncle Lou once took the dog to have its fur cut short in a particularly hot summer. The dog would not go outside until his fur grew back, he was so self conscious about losing his luxurious coat. He also waited for my uncle to go to sleep and then crept up on him and bit him hard in the behind as payback.

Growing up in the late 20's and 30's in NYC had its challenges. Anti-Semitism was very rampant back then. A Nazi Bund Hall opened just up the street and it made my mother very nervous to walk past them. As a young girl someone called her a "dirty Jew." She ran to my Grandmother showing that her dress was clean and questioning the remark. At school my uncle was short and skinny and was a target for bullies. One boy, a large kid of Polish descent, would beat him up regularly. Finally my uncle told him "Some day I'm going to be a doctor and you will need to see me for help. When that day happens I will put you under anesthesia and cut your testicles off." The bully backed down.

My uncle did become a physician who specialized in psychiatry. He and my Aunt Eugenia Lunsky, and their children Ann, Ben and Lori Lunsky moved to Los Angeles and eventually my parents, older brothers and grandmother Esther followed them to California in 1957.

I asked my grandmother how the family ended up in New York City when she and her numerous brothers were born and raised in Massachusetts? Eventually the story surfaced that a brother she was very close to, saw a member of an Irish gang beating an elderly Jewish man around 1908. My great uncle, known for his temper, hit the punk on the head with a piece of lumber until he collapsed. Fearing that the man would die and police retribution would be swift, the entire family packed up and moved to New York City overnight.

Growing up I was fortunate to be born later in life to my parents. My oldest brother Nathan was born to my parents in 1950 and my brother Mark followed in 1953. I was the 'surprise' of the family born in 1965. I am the only native Californian in the family and have never experienced snow.

I feel very blessed to have been raised by a loving family of an older generation than my friend's families. I learned about the Great Depression and my mother's fears listening to radio reports as a child, of families having to give up their children for lack of food and shelter. My grandmother Esther talked about losing a brother to the Spanish Flu pandemic after WW1 and how virtually all families suffered losses. My great uncle Hymie Morse described seeing the 1910 appearance of Halley's Comet in the dark skies of New York.

My Dad, Robert Spero, was a World War Two U.S. Navy combat veteran. He had joined the Navy the day after the December 7, 1941 attack on Pearl Harbor. As a teenager and young adult I would accompany my father to Veterans of Foreign Wars and American Legion events where I got to know many members of the 'Greatest Generation' as well as Korean and Vietnam war veterans. I had many long talks with those gentlemen about what it was like to be at Normandy, France on D-Day June 6, 1944. I learned about the Battle of the Bulge, Iwo Jima, Guadalcanal, and the other deadly battlefields.

My Dad told me about liberating the starving victims in Japanese POW camps in the Phillipines. I heard about his memory of seeing the brilliant flash of the Hiroshima atomic bomb from 300 miles away on August 6th, 1945. Some aspects of the war were too painful for him to discuss. He had nightmares of his work removing corpses from the sunken ships at Pearl Harbor that would awaken him at night with screams throughout the 1970's. I am in awe of the sacrifices and decency of that generation.

My grandmother was quite feisty and stood up for herself and her family without hesitation. She and my mother both taught me to have faith that God would get us through anything life could throw at us. They both had a good sense of humor.

On my dad's side, his mother, my grandmother Hannah, and grandfather George Spero, both of blessed memory, lived in a brownstone apartment building in Astoria, Long Island. My grandmother Hannah ran a greeting card shop. My grandfather was involved with the US Navy and worked on a project to make warships out of concrete. The idea sounded good on paper but problems developed and the ships sank like a brick. My older brothers got to know Grandpa George, whom I am named after. He took them to Disneyland when it first opened in Anaheim, California. When my Dad was a kid, Grandpa George drove an early 1920's Chevrolet and I have a photo of my Dad as a kid in a pond with the old Chevy parked behind him. My father remembered the first time he saw a color movie with my grandfather, The Wizard of Oz, which played Radio City Music Hall in 1939 and really impressed him. He also saw Babe Ruth play in Yankee Stadium.

My father had a wealthy Uncle Ralph who owned a hotel in Atlantic City on the Boardwalk. My Dad would work summers as an elevator operator there. He told me that a lot of the Gangsters of the 1920's and 1930's would stay there and they tipped him really well. He used to enjoy rides in his Uncle's 16-cylinder Pierce Arrow automobiles, which cost more than a house back then,

My parents loved to tell the story of how they met in late December 1945. Although they grew up near each other and knew some of the same people, they had never met. My mother was five years younger than my father and looked much younger than her true age. One time a date complained when she ordered a glass of milk on a date that she was making him look like a pedophile!

Each of them was going to a friend's wedding and had just boarded a subway train. My father was accompanying a female neighbor to the wedding but not as a date. My Dad had just been discharged from the U.S. Navy and was still in uniform. He saw my mother and immediately came to sit by her and talk with her. My mother was quite shocked and horrified because she thought he was leaving his wife or girlfriend alone to hit on her. Eventually he explained that he had no relationship with the woman and they really connected. They agreed to go on a first date on New Year's Eve to Times Square to welcome 1946. There was a huge crowd that year and extreme jubilation that the war had been won. They continued to date until their marriage on August 16, 1947.

Many businesses started and failed in that first year after WW2. My father had and lost 12 jobs that first year as businesses opened and closed. On one job he served as a late night usher at a movie theater on Steinway Street. He was tired from his day job doing electronics and fell asleep. While he snored vandals cut apart the upholstery of dozens of theater seats. The job ended very soon after that.

My grandmother Esther reassured my mother that Bob was a hard worker and would eventually land a good job. My mother worked for a fine men's clothing store and proudly told me how she successfully negotiated a raise of a nickel more per hour. As a radioman in the Navy my Dad learned about electronics. During the war early radar antennas were not motorized. He sometimes had to climb the masts to hand crank the antennas while Japanese fighter pilots were trying to shoot up and kamikaze into his ship. He told me that really wasn't a good place to be at those moments. He went to work in 1947 making televisions and radios.

One company only had him wiring a certain part of a circuit board. He was not told what the final product was. My Dad almost never got ill, but he did miss a few days of work while sick with the flu at that job. During that time, the Feds raided the business and arrested all there for making illegal slot machines. His being sick spared him from going through that. He eventually got a job in aerospace and worked for McDonnell Douglas for many years. One of his proudest achievements was when he was selected to wire panels for the Skylab satellite.

Dad was not really demonstrative but I knew he loved my brothers and I. We went fishing once off the rock jetty at the Long Beach Naval Station where he worked. He would drive me to Hebrew High School classes on Tuesday night and we had a tradition of getting Del Taco tacos afterwards and talking.

Despite his father's Chevrolet, my Dad was a Ford man and he loved the large station wagons made by Ford and Mercury. Most of my childhood memories are of taking trips in the huge old wagons, often from the rear jump seats with the tailgate window down.

Dad gave me his 1969 Ford Country Sedan station wagon when I got my driver's license in 1981. He taught me to drive in that 21' long, wide wagon. The car had the headliner held in place with silver duct tape. The vinyl bench seat was coming apart at the seams and metal springs would jab me in the rear end. I adored that car and loved the powerful 390 V8 engine. I first learned to work on old cars with that wagon. When it finally rusted out years later I wept to see it go.

One family trip to Desert Hot springs in the mid 1970's was particularly memorable. We would go out there each winter to stay at a motel for a couple of nights and enjoy the hot springs. I loved seeing Claude Bell's roadside Dinosaurs, off Highway 10 in Cabazon, CA by the Wheel Inn with its huge lighted "EAT" sign.

This one time, something happened to the radiator and the car overheated in an area called the Badlands. We had some water and coolant but not enough to fill the huge radiator. There were no cell-phones back then and no pay phone for miles. My father called me and my older brothers to gather around. He held out the water container and asked us to "do our duty as men." He then proceeded to urinate his own special 'yellow coolant' into the container and thanked each of us for contributing whatever we could as well. It actually worked well enough to get us to Desert Hot Springs where he had the problem repaired.

We told that story at Dad's funeral in 2005 and I still smile thinking of it. My friend Menashe Cohen and I once worked on the 4bbl carburetor of the '69 Ford wagon while still in high school. A glob of gasoline made it through to the hot muffler which exploded and flew smoking and skittering across four lanes of Torrance Blvd., the main street in town. Thankfully nobody was hurt. Menashe thought my father would be angry, as the car now sounded like an earsplitting race car with open exhaust, but Dad just laughed and said he knew we would get it fixed.

One time when I was 16, my grandmother Esther asked me to switch places with her in her nursing home wheelchair. I would ride and she would push. The double takes done by the nurses were fun to see.

Another time I was wheeling her outside for a walk around the block on a nice day. As we passed the nursing station, her young nurse was kissing her boyfriend who was enjoying a nice feel. Grandma waited until we were nearly past them and then asked 'Does your mother know what you are doing with *him?'*

The nurse screamed and said *'Mrs. Lunsky, I didn't know that you could talk!'* while my grandmother laughed. She was devoutly religious, always lighting Shabbat candles weekly and attending as many synagogue services as she could. She taught me how to cook a brisket of beef, rubbing it with spices such that the meat could not be seen. It was delicious and tender. She always carried some hard candy in her purse to offer to me.

My oldest brother Nathan was unable to drive and was living in a Board and Care home in Norwalk. He learned to master the RTD bus lines and once took twelve buses to see our grandmother, who lived at the time in Culver City, which she appreciated.

It was through my grandmother Esther that I learned about the impact a caring attitude can have. She was seeing a traditional Asian man as her doctor. Once, when she was in her early 90's, he said *'Mrs. Lunsky I am going to miss you.'* Clearly he meant when she was dead, as she well knew. She asked him *'Where are you going that you will miss me?'* He was too embarrassed to answer her.

We switched doctors to Dr. Harry Blackman, M.D. in Los Angeles. Dr. Blackman was a Jewish man who was near retirement age. He knew how to deal with elderly Jewish women.

When my parents mentioned that they were worried that my grandmother would sit for hours with her eyes shut, he had a solution. He said *'Mrs. Lunsky, if you sit with your eyes closed, someone will steal your purse from you.'* Problem solved as nobody was going to steal her purse if she could prevent it! As the only girl in a family with 11 boys she was a tomboy, which was not the norm for the early 20th century. She wouldn't hesitate to tell somebody to 'go to hell' when necessary and stood up for herself and her family her entire life.

My mother had a wide happy smile and laugh and very warm brown eyes. As a child she would read with me daily and instilled a love of learning. I don't think she ever had an enemy in her life as she could befriend anyone. I learned her recipe for Chicken Matzo Ball Soup at a young age, which she often made for guests and family gatherings. In her memory I make it for each service at our home.

Mom was a bookkeeper in the 1970's for California Jupiter Corporation, a Japanese company based in Torrance, California. My father was not at all pleased that she was working for a Japanese firm, given his experiences in World War Two. The employers were nice, although Mom thought it a bit strange to have to bow before a photograph of Emperor Hirohito as well as the company President in Japan each morning and tell each of them her work goals for the day. One time in 1972 some high corporate executives visited Torrance from Japan. My Dad agreed to be nice to them and they came over for dinner.

Chicken Matzo Ball Soup was an immediate success. I was around 7 years old. My parents asked me to play something for them on my clarinet and I was surprised when the executive asked if he could borrow the instrument and he played a beautiful Japanese melody for us. Things got a little dicey when the topic of the war came up and it turned out that the executive had some role in the planning or execution of the Pearl Harbor attack. Still, the evening ended well. When my mother was hospitalized for a gallbladder attack and surgery, the company employees folded 1000 origami cranes for her and made a hanging display of them as a get well gift. She always treasured that.

My Dad started having shakiness and some memory issues by 1978. Just before my Bar Mitzvah the following year he was given a devastating prognosis that he probably had Alzheimer's and would not live past six months. Mom went with me to the synagogue and asked Rabbi Kahane's permission for her to say a silent prayer before the open Ark. He gave her permission, she opened the ark and poured her heart out to God. God was listening because my father's condition did not significantly worsen until a year or so before his death in 2005.

Dad was well liked at the Long Beach Naval Shipyard where he was a tool crib operator for eighteen years after being laid off just before reaching full retirement from McDonnell Douglas. He could be grumpy at times and a little like Archie Bunker about things, but he had some very good friends there.

Our entire family was invited to his retirement luncheon hosted by his coworkers. They had saved some wood from the surrender deck of the U.S.S. Missouri battleship, which the shipyard had refurbished. They made a plaque out of the wood and presented it to him. He always treasured that. My parents had friends of all faiths, races and cultural traditions.

Truly anything good that I have managed to accomplish in my life is due to them and the good examples and moral values they practiced.

Sheryl and the kids and I have created some unique family memories as well. After months of completing adoption paperwork and taking parenting classes we were very excited about meeting our children in person.

I think we had some culture shock when we landed in Hanoi, Vietnam. The soldiers at the airport wore Soviet style uniforms and carried AK-47 rifles.

Our trip through the countryside into Hanoi revealed a very beautiful and green country. Nice old Chinese and French architecture buildings were mixed with modern ones. People's homes ran the gamut from very modern to little more than shacks.

Everywhere people rode scooters and motorcycles! We would see a family of six riding atop a 50cc scooter, often carrying substantial loads.

The Old Quarter of Hanoi was filled with throngs of people and cars and scooters constantly honking each other. The noise level reminded me of my visits to Manhattan.

Small shops were everywhere with certain businesses located on certain streets. You would go to one street for metal wares, another for mattresses, musical instruments or toys. The food was superb with Vietnamese, Chinese, French and western cuisine. In the mornings I enjoyed Pho rice noodle soup with fresh baguettes while the local news was broadcast via loudspeakers to the city. While many are poor in Vietnam they have one of the highest literacy rates in the world. Many people spoke several languages and were very pleasant to interact with.

Our first meeting with our kids reduced us to tears of joy. My fears that they might be frightened by my beard were baseless. Holding them I was sure that Sheryl's Dad and my parent's souls were with us rejoicing. My alma mater, Whittier College School of Law, donated a large box of infant and toddler t-shirts and sweatshirts to give to the orphanage, Ba Vi Social Protection Center #5. I wonder how many Vietnamese infants are still using those law school shirts?

On our trip back to the hotel the babies, James 7 months and Esther 9 ½ months old watched passing scooters and motorcycles with fascination. My beard was tugged and played with. I was in disbelief that we had been entrusted with two infants and was scared silly of doing something wrong. Other than raising a basset hound from puppyhood I was not used to dealing with babies. We quickly mastered bottle feedings and diapers. I am grateful to my in-laws for their good advice and assistance at every step of the journey.

At age 9 ½ months Esther was fearless. She could stand on her own and walk around the hotel room holding onto furniture. James needed to learn to crawl but loved being held. We bought a saucer shaped walking toy that helped to build up his legs.

We have so many good memories from our five weeks there. People were friendly and many spoke English. Everyone we met would stop to talk or play with the kids. We took the kids to a traditional water puppet theater with live musicians and colorful puppets.

I was struck at how young the average age seemed to be. In restaurants the waitresses, in their 20's, would hold and play with the babies while we ate. I had been concerned about how we would be received as Americans in Hanoi, but the war didn't present any issues. A fellow about my age remembered B-52 bombings in the 70's that nearly killed him, yet told me he had a dream of coming to the United States. I would hope if Americans are visiting Iraq or Afghanistan forty years from now that they would be welcomed in the same manner.

An elderly woman, who had to be 100 years old, gave the children a special blessing and corrected my way of holding them and giving the kids a bottle. An entourage with her nodded encouragingly. I love the way Vietnamese culture has tremendous respect for elders and wish we had more of that in the USA. God knows I welcomed the old woman's advice!

In Vietnamese culture all babies have to have a hat on their head when outdoors no matter the temperature. To do otherwise would be shocking and offensive to the public. We tried to keep hats on our kids' heads but they loved taking them off. Sheryl would show the hat to anyone looking at us with a frown to say 'here it is, we have it, they just won't wear it!'

We each went through bouts of stomach bugs and poor James struggled with the pneumonia, although he was always cheerful. An international S.O.S. clinic in downtown Hanoi had the needed antibiotics and were very caring. Leaving Vietnam we were waiting in the Business Class airport lounge to board our flight. We thought we would let the babies crawl on the floor by us. Just then we saw a huge rat going from table to table looking for scraps. I mentioned it to the lounge employee who said yes, the rat is friendly and is looking for food. We kept the kids in our laps and said maybe the first class lounge has a squirrel or better class of rodent!

Back at home, the synagogue welcomed the children with open arms. Before we left for Vietnam the congregation had a wonderful baby shower for us and we had everything set up and waiting for our return. While I missed my parents terribly, all of the seniors would take turns holding and playing with the babies as did the religious school kids. One Friday night comes to mind where James was being held and smiling but would start to cry if put down. Two ladies were taking turns holding him. Esther was scooting around the room. While I was leading a fairly serious prayer from my podium people started laughing. I didn't know what was funny until Sheryl came racing up and scooped up Esther from in front of the podium where she decided to cast off her diaper and shirt and go streaking.

I have so many wonderful memories with the children and love watching them grow into the sweet eight year olds they have become.

They are as close as twins with each other and we thank God for making us a family every night. I recently bought an old Ford station wagon like my father's and look forward to taking a family vacation in it with Sheryl and the kids.

Chapter 22 - My Mom's Recipe For Chicken Matzo Ball Soup: a.k.a. Jewish Penicillin

Here is the way I learned it from my maternal grandmother, Esther Lunsky, and from my Mom Pearl Spero, of blessed memory, who refined the recipe as it is stated here. It was made for every holiday dinner and when any of us were sick. I call my at home congregation the Matzo Ball Minyan and serve this soup after each service. You will need:

Manischewitz brand Matzo Ball and Soup mix, sold in the kosher foods aisle of Albertson's and Ralphs and other supermarkets. Note that this combo box has a very different tasting and lighter Matzo ball recipe than their box with just matzo ball mix in it. I have never been able to duplicate the taste with any other brand or with the other Manischewitz mix. For 10-12 people I make two batches at once, requiring two boxes. I will give the recipe for one box; just double everything for the bigger batch.

2 large eggs.

2 tablespoons Wesson oil or other vegetable or canola oil. It can also be made with olive oil but has a slightly different taste.

1 or 2 chicken half breasts, preferably with ribs and skin.

1 package of peeled fresh baby carrots or several large carrots peeled and chopped into 1/2" – 1" pieces. You can also use a water packed container of 50/50 pre-peeled carrots and celery stalks from the produce aisle to save some time, just slice them into 1/2" – 1" pieces.

Several celery stalks sliced into 1/2" pieces unless using the pre-pack container with the carrots.

One medium yellow onion, quartered. (Don't use the pre-chopped or sliced onion as it won't taste the same). For a double recipe use one large onion.

Fresh parsley. - My mom and I almost always forgot to add this to the cooked soup, sort of a family tradition of memory loss, but it tastes good with it added.

Put 2 1/2 quarts (10 cups) of water into a large pot. You can add an extra cup or two and it still tastes great and gives a little more soup when it is cooked. Whisk in the soup mix packet to the cold water. You can do this with a fork also if you don't have a whisk.

Add the chicken breasts and onion at this time. Cover and cook over a medium heat until soup is boiling, and then add the carrots and celery.

Boil slowly uncovered on a low to medium heat until chicken is cooked through - about 45 minutes.

While chicken soup is cooking break two eggs into a medium bowl and whisk in the oil, or blend them with a fork. Add the matzo ball mix and stir thoroughly. Refrigerate for at least 15 minutes.

When soup is boiling and the chicken is cooked, take matzo ball mix from the refrigerator and stir again. It will be very thick and sticky. Wet your hands and don't dry them. Pick up a little of the mixture and roll it into a half inch ball between your palms. Drop very carefully, each ball individually into the boiling soup. You may need to re-wet your hands a few times to get this done. The matzo balls will sink and then rise to the surface turning white and getting bigger. After dropping in all of the uncooked matzo balls cover the pot tightly and lower the heat to a simmer. Cook another 20 minutes covered and simmering. Uncover, remove from heat and enjoy! I usually discard the chicken skin and remove and slice the chicken from the bones and re-add it to the soup. This is when you would add the parsley.

You can make this a day in advance, just let it cool and then refrigerate the entire pot. You can skim the fat off the cooled soup if you wish but it tastes better with some in the soup. The flavors will get more blended overnight. Reheat covered on a low heat until hot and serve.

Chapter 23 - Our *Bashert* Moment – Meeting and Marrying Sheryl Lynn Joiner, The Love Of My Life.

Bashert is a Yiddish word used to describe a Divinely intended match. Both Sheryl and I had experienced enough miserable dating horrors in our lives to recognize when something good finally came along.

By age 37 I thought I had a better chance of being attacked by a Great White Shark than I did of meeting my soul-mate. I was resigned to enjoying my professional life and then living in a single wide trailer in the desert with a basset hound for company.

Then I heard about J-Date, an online Jewish dating website. For a nominal cost I created a dating profile citing my religious observance preferences and the fact that outside of my law job I enjoyed riding my Harley, spending time with my dog, as well as reading, music, cooking and fixing up and driving classic cars.

Whatever algorithms J-Date uses, they suggested I might like to contact a woman using the profile name 'Bibliophile.' Bibliophile had not posted a photo of herself but described a religious observance level like mine and that she was a librarian with a love of cats and a pet mouse named Mazal. We started emailing each other and I was immediately impressed by her wonderful use of English and down to earth attitude.

We started talking by telephone and finally arranged a first date on March 16, 2002 at the Daily Grill restaurant in Irvine, CA near her Pepperdine University library job. We would meet after she left work for dinner. It was a public enough place that if either of us showed up with chainsaws or other weapons we wouldn't be alone.

To prepare, I bought some cat treats for Fortune and mouse treats for Mazal. I intended to also buy a rose to give to her. The flower lady at the market asked me why I wanted a rose and I told her about our date. *'Don't buy a rose, show some creativity!'* she said. She then guided me to her display of Gerber daisy flowers. These were huge and brightly colored. I had my doubts but bought a large orange one on a long stalk and had my brown paper bag filled with pet treats.

Back then I had two vehicles. A 2001 Harley Davidson Heritage Springer Softail motorcycle in deep metallic blue and silver and a jet black 1998 BMW Z3 convertible, the first luxury car I bought after becoming a lawyer. I chose the Z3 and drove to the restaurant. Sheryl was there in a blue dress as promised and I was very taken by her.

Sheryl saw me coming in with a large ridiculous orange flower and a brown paper bag. 'Oh no' she thought to herself, 'he packed his own dinner to the restaurant!' When she learned that the bag had cat and mouse goodies she was very pleased and later told me that impressed her greatly that I would think about her pets on our first date. Sheryl graciously accepted the daisy although I learned much later that a rose would have been her preference.

We had a wonderful meal and good conversation and I was seeing future marriage potential by the time we got our check. Having established that I wasn't a psychopath, or at least not an *obvious* psychopath, we went together in the convertible to a nearby bookstore. We started speaking every day by phone and dating several times per week. I visited her library and saw how she guided graduate students and professors in finding reference materials on a large variety of subjects. She is a great librarian.

One evening in late April I met her at the Pepperdine University library in Irvine on my Harley and brought along a helmet for Sheryl. Some biker friends of mine were celebrating a 25th wedding anniversary and vow renewal ceremony at their home in Orange County and we planned on riding there together.

Before we left, Sheryl approached me and asked me to marry

her! I absolutely vapor locked. I stammered and was barely able to speak. While I was falling very much in love with Sheryl we had only known each other 6 weeks. I thought it would be better to hold off on getting engaged for at least a few more months. A prior dating experience left me gun-shy when my former date underwent a radical personality change after six months. To this day I regret not accepting Sheryl's proposal right on the spot that night. At least I knew what her thoughts were and that she was open to marriage!

We rode to the party, which was in a backyard full of motorcyclists. The food line was long but I waited to get food for us while Sheryl held our places at a table in the yard.

It was then that a contingent from the local "Dykes On Bikes" chapter arrived. This is a Harley riding organization of lesbians who are active in LGBT community matters. A lovely redheaded lady sat across from Sheryl. There was a dish of Hershey's Kisses on the table. She asked Sheryl 'Please pass me a kiss, unless *YOU* would like to give me one yourself.' Sheryl quickly passed her the bowl of chocolates. I couldn't believe it, I left for three minutes and the lesbians descended on her. Sheryl told me jokingly, with a smile, that she bet *'that lady wouldn't have vapor locked on my proposal, and she also rode a sweet looking Harley as well.'* I was ready to crawl under the table.

One thing I liked about Sheryl right from the start, besides her sense of humor and brilliance, was her leather motorcycle jacket. It was soft and worn in the right places and looked great on her. I loved riding the Harley with her holding on behind me. I asked how she came to buy a motorcycle jacket since she didn't ride a motorcycle herself. She smiled and told me her Rabbis had been telling her to ditch the jacket *'as no man will want to marry a woman wearing one.'* They were dead wrong about that and admitted it to Sheryl and I at our wedding. God always knows best!

I made up my mind to propose to her by late May. We agreed that her Dad would be very pleased if I flew out to Texas to meet her parents and ask her father's permission to propose marriage. I spoke privately with her Dad and he gave me his blessing. My mother gave me my grandmother Esther's engagement diamond and I had it set into a simple Platinum band for Sheryl. On May 31st, my 37th birthday, I got down on one knee and asked her hand in marriage. When Sheryl saw me getting on one knee she thought maybe one of her Mom's cats had gotten sick under the table. She was relieved that wasn't the case and gladly accepted my proposal, as I should have accepted hers a month and a half earlier. Jewish guilt is real and I will bear this regret for life. But I was thrilled that we were engaged.

We decided to marry on December 1, 2002 at her Rabbi's synagogue, B'nei Tzedek, in Fountain Valley. Both of her teachers, Rabbi Stephen Einstein and Rabbi Bernie King, of blessed memory, officiated. It was also my mother's 76th birthday and my ten year anniversary of being sworn in as an attorney. Sheryl had converted to Judaism years before meeting me. Both Rabbi Einstein and Rabbi King were her teachers. Trust me, they put me through a grilling to make sure that I was the right guy for Sheryl!

Thankfully both sets of parents were alive and present at the wedding. Sheryl's dad was fighting terminal melanoma cancer and both of my parents had some serious health issues. They all had a great time at the wedding as did we. In the eleven and a half years since then we have built quite a life together. We helped each other through the passing of her father and my parents, the loss of many good friends and several beloved pets. Sheryl encouraged me to pursue my dream of becoming ordained as a Rabbi. I studied very intensively for a year to prepare for the *Beit Din*. Had it not been for Sheryl's love and encouragement I might never have done so.

As a librarian she also owned a lot of books! Of the 150 titles that were required reading by the seminary, Sheryl already had 148 of them, organized and labeled using the Library of Congress cataloging system. Indeed, when we bought our home she went from a 600 square foot apartment in Fullerton to a 2000 square foot house in Torrance. My Aunt Eugenia thought we would be rattling around like two peas in a can in our home. After Sheryl's 17 bookcases were moved into the house, it no longer felt empty. She has been a wonderful wife, an outstanding Mom to our kids and a dedicated *Rebbetzin* – a Rabbi's wife, to our congregants and others in need of spiritual guidance. Before meeting Sheryl I could not imagine the life we have together. She is truly the love of my life. Hopefully God will permit us to grow old together.

CHAPTER 24 - DOES THE BODY SIN OR THE SOUL?

I would like to relate a famous rabbinic parable, called a *Midrash*, about whether we are more subject to the will of our souls or our bodies.

From the Talmud tractate Sanhedrin 91a-b

'Antoninus said to Rabbi Judah HaNassi: The body and the soul can each absolve themselves from judgment. The body can say: 'It is the soul who has sinned. Why, from the day it left me, I lie like a dumb stone in the grave!' And the soul can say: 'It's the body who transgressed. From the day I departed from it, I fly about in the air like a bird!'

Said Rabbi Judah: I will tell you a parable.

Once there was a king who had a beautiful orchard with splendid figs. He appointed two watchmen for his orchard. One watchman was lame, and the other one was blind.

One day the lame man said to the blind man: 'I see beautiful figs in the orchard. Come, I will ride on your shoulders, and we'll take them and eat them.' So the lame man rode on the shoulders of the blind man, and they took the fruits and ate them.

Some time after, the owner of the orchard came and inquired of them, 'Where are those beautiful figs?' The lame man replied, 'Have I feet to walk with?' The blind man replied, 'Have I eyes to see with?'

What did the king do? He placed the lame watchman on the shoulders of the blind watchman, and judged them together.'

So too, we are creatures of both the body and the spirit. It can be hard to find a good balance in our lives, yet we must be kind to both body and soul to have a fulfilling and complete life. To be spiritual but not act on that spirituality is comparable to a fruit laden tree where the fruit goes to waste. To be physically active but not have time for the spirit is like an orange with neither much smell nor taste. Find the middle path, between extremes, and life will be satisfying and complete.

Chapter 25 - What is The Reason for The Jewish Star?

Have you ever wondered about why the Jewish star is shaped the way it is? It is a six pointed star with one point pointing upward, one pointing downward and two facing each side. Basically it is two equilateral triangles balanced upon each other. In Hebrew we call this the *Magen David*, literally the *Shield of David*. Tradition says that King David had this emblem on his shield when he went into battle.

It is a sign of the balance King David sought. He was very spiritual, authoring many Psalms to God, but also well grounded in the world. He tried to walk a path of moderation without going to the extreme in any situation.

I think the Star of David is a good focusing tool to use in meditation. Where are we in life? What changes do we need to bring about to improve our lives? Do we read and study worthwhile things? Do we allow time to listen to beautiful music and view art? Do we attend religious services and think about the needs of others? Are we so involved in these things that our weight and heath is out of control? Can we adjust our diet to eat better and find time for exercise? Do we do at least one act of kindness for another each day? Remember that to change direction, we simply have to turn ourselves just a little bit and follow the new path.

Chapter 26 - A Few Words About Some Congregants

My dear friend and congregant Joanie Shulman, who helped edit this book, lost her husband Gus a few years ago after a long and happy marriage. They had done quite a bit of traveling and had many friends. She could have been embittered by his passing and lived in sadness, but she chose another path. Joanie is very involved with her relatives and friends. A retired school teacher, she is also very computer savvy and sends me and her friends a 'Daily Chuckle' by email which always gives me a lift. Even though she has some health challenges, she doesn't let them interfere with making personal connections with others. Her love of books and cats and brilliant mind has endeared her to Sheryl and me. I believe she is the only person I know who can appreciate a really good cup of coffee or espresso more than I.

Judy Giss, of blessed memory, was another person who embraced life with a joyous positive attitude. Judy was a Christian who was active in the Manhattan Beach Community Church for many decades. She was married to Rabbi Ken Giss, who was the best man at my wedding. They were realtors who were very well known and active in charitable causes. Judy and Ken would visit virtually every synagogue in the South Bay and were welcomed everywhere. Even the local Hasidim welcomed Judy and she used to teach the girls and women the beautiful melody for the Hebrew blessings for the Shabbat candles. She would also turn on and off lights and adjust the thermostat for them on Shabbat when traditional Jews do not do such things.

Judy would take copious notes on each sermon she heard. Her photographs at all events she attended and gift photo albums after the event were treasures. She never forgot a birthday or anniversary and often wrote cards to all.

Very few of us knew that Judy was battling an aggressive cancer for a number of years. She would dress up and wear beautiful hats to services and always had a caring smile. She and Ken would sit with me when my parents had their own surgeries and were always concerned and involved with my family life. Literally hundreds of people of many faiths attended Judy's funeral service. She touched so many lives, leaving behind a positive example and loving memories for each of us to follow and treasure. I know she is standing in the blazing light of God's love, in eternal joy.

Chapter 27 - Some Weird Rabbinic Stories From Over The Years

As a Rabbi I have fielded my share of unusual calls over the years. One Passover Eve a lady called me absolutely frantic, asking where she could get some lamb's blood? I asked her why she wanted such a thing? She told me *'to paint the doorposts of my house so that the Angel of Death will pass over my household.'* The poor woman thought that the command to Moses and the Israelites on the night of the tenth plague in Egypt, some 3,250 years ago was an ongoing commandment.

I reassured her that no blood was needed. Just read the Passover *hagaddah*, the special service booklet for the holiday, and attend a Passover Seder if possible. I further pointed out that if the firstborn died every year on Passover Eve it would be quite a yearly news story and people would invest in lamb's blood futures every spring.

As a law student doing an internship with Torrance City Prosecutor's Office, which turned into my first law job as an attorney, I had a bizarre occurrence. My boss Jesse placed a police report in front of me. I would review these reports to determine what criminal charges, if any, should be filed.

I was told *'These are your people, deal with this."* I cringed wondering what some Jew had done. When a Jewish person turns to a life of crime, in my experience it is a major crime! My Uncle, Dr. Louis Lunsky, once told me he thought the infamous mobster Meyer Lansky was a distant relative.

The police report stated that an officer was dispatched to a house on Beryl Street, near the Redondo Beach city border because a neighbor thought a child was being abused and was screaming very loudly. The police got there just in time to find several bearded men, dressed in white robes, who had just slaughtered a lamb and were offering it as a burnt sacrifice on a stone altar in their Torrance, CA backyard. The men spoke very little English but explained to the police that it is for the Passover observance. This shocked me as Jews have not sacrificed lambs or any other creatures since the Fall of the Second Temple in Jerusalem in the year 70!

I decided to call the homeowner personally. To my great surprise he answered me not in Hebrew but in the ancient language of Aramaic. I know Aramaic as a result of my studies. Other than in public prayers and ancient texts I was not aware that anyone still spoke it as a living language. I told him that Jews do not kill lambs for Passover so what was he doing? He told me that is true, but his family is a descendant of Laban the Aramean, Patriarch Jacob's uncle. The Arameans broke off from the Jews after the Exodus from Egypt but still worship God in the most ancient way. I was amazed to learn that the largest population of Arameans in the world is now in Southern California, in addition to a group in Israel.

I suggested that in the future he and his family should drive out into the desert to do this as there are laws against butchering living animals at home in Torrance. Under the First Amendment of the United States Constitution they have the right to worship as their ancestors have done for millennia. I recommended that no charges be filed against them and found the entire encounter to be somewhat surreal and fascinating.

In seminary I had to learn the basics of most of the world's faiths. This included Santeria, a form of Voodoo prevalent in South America that mimics Roman Catholic services but adds the slaughter of chickens and goats as dark boons to the entities they worship. I asked Rabbi Gelberman when on earth I would ever have to interact with such a thing, as my mind felt violated just by reading about their offerings. Rabbi Gelberman smiled and said 'You never know when, but when the time comes, knowledge is invaluable.'

One night a couple came to see me about getting married. The groom was an older gentleman who was raised Jewish. The bride was a young and stunning Brazilian woman who wanted to convert to Judaism. In discussing conversion I asked about her family's religious practices. She told me she was Roman Catholic 'but didn't like the way the Church hurt the animals.'

I asked her what she meant as the only Church interaction with animals I was aware of, is sprinkling them with holy water for a special blessing. She said the chickens and the goats. I described some of the abominations I had learned about Santeria and she said yes, that is what was done. The bride came from a small village in Southern Brazil that was remote.

In centuries past, the Santeria worshippers would make it look like they had given up their pagan ways and accepted Spanish Catholicism. Their leaders dressed as priests and their churches had crucifixes and candles. This was done so that the Conquistadors wouldn't slaughter them all as heretics.

I told her that before she undertook conversion to Judaism I wanted her to meet with an actual Roman Catholic parish priest locally, to really learn about Catholicism before abandoning it. She was very grateful. I never saw them again but hope all worked out well for them.

On the afternoon of *Rosh Hashana*, the Jewish New Year, we do a service by a body of water called *Tashlikh*. This is Hebrew for "casting away" and involves symbolically casting some bread crumbs into a body of water with fish in it, to represent all of the things we want to change about our lives and not carry forward into the new year. My practice is to assemble a group by the ocean in late afternoon and do the ceremony. One year I wore a prayer shawl I made myself years earlier. A friend, Gary Frank, taught a class on designing and making a personalized tallit. It was made of wool out of a Scottish tartan fabric. I added a collar and corners from a *tallit* that was in bad shape and hand knotted the special *tzittzit* fringes which turn a piece of cloth into a Tallit.

We said some *Tashlikh* prayers and songs and then separated to cast off some crumbs to the waiting fish and seagulls. An elderly gentleman with a strong Scottish brogue came up to me, clapped me on the shoulder, and said *'What a foyne service ye led, laddie, just like me brother's.'* Amazed to find a Scottish Jew, I said "Your brother did *Tashlikh* like we just did?" *"Aye, he was buried at sea too.'* I quickly explained that we were not casting off human ashes but rather bread crumbs from the pier and explained the service. In the future I only used my tartan tallit at home!

After Proposition 8, California's ban on same sex marriages, was overturned by the Court, I had the honor of officiating at both gay and lesbian weddings. In the past I could do "commitment" ceremonies but wasn't allowed to declare the couples legally married under state law.

I was thrilled to officiate at a wedding for two ladies in the gorgeous Santa Ynez Valley in Central California. They were very much in love and made a good couple. One lady was Jewish and her family had come to America from Russia. The other lady hailed from South America. Both of their families were supportive and attended the wedding.

The Russian grandmother and I spoke for awhile. She had survived both the Nazis and the Soviet Union. She was very pleased to have a Rabbi officiate at the wedding but was also sad. I asked why was she sad? She told me she loved her granddaughter and the lady she was marrying, but had always had a dream of having great grandchildren. How could that be possible with two women?

I had talked about this with the wedding couple and knew they were anxious to explore adoption as a way to form a family. I told the grandmother that with adoption and even medical fertility options, I was quite sure that she would be holding a baby or two before too long. This made her smile and truly be joyous at the wedding. The non-Jewish mother also spoke with me. I congratulated her on the wedding and pointed out that she now had a Jewish doctor in the family. She was indeed pleased by the thought that her brilliant and beautiful daughter was marrying a doctor! It was one of the happiest weddings at which I have ever officiated.

Certain cultural beliefs can also have an impact on a couple's life. I officiated at an outdoor wedding for a Jewish couple in

Palos Verdes' famous La Venta Inn which has an amazing view of the Los Angeles basin from the top of the Palos Verdes Peninsula. The groom was an American Jewish guy with ancestors from Eastern Europe. The bride was born in Tunisia and followed Sephardic Jewish customs. Her parents flew in from Tunisia and spoke beautiful French. The bride followed Tunisian custom and wore a gorgeous red bridal gown. White is the color of death in their tradition so red is the norm.

All went well in the ceremony until a gigantic horsefly kamikazied into the Kiddush cup of wine to be shared by the couple. That fly burned in so hard he sent wine splashing up a few feet away from the cup. I interrupted the ceremony to request that a wedding coordinator please wash out and refill the cup.

It was then that I saw the agitation and distress among the bride's family. I could not understand French and asked the bride to please translate for me. She told me her parents thought that this was an evil sign as flies represent demonic forces. I thought to myself 'no, that is birds, crows in particular' but tried to calm the situation down. I explained that in America a fly is just an insect and this one found the Manischewitz to be so delicious he dove face first into it to join in the celebration. People laughed and with a clean cup of wine we continued. I learned a lesson from that always to cover the kiddush cup with cling wrap in future outdoor ceremonies or to pour directly from the bottle or decanter just before making the blessing.

Chapter 28 - The Hardest And Most Joyous Days In My Rabbinic Work

The most difficult service at which I have ever officiated, was for a young Israeli woman, a mother and wife, murdered by a homicide bomber's explosive death. My synagogue's Hebrew school teacher, an Israeli woman, came to me with the news of her niece's murder in Israel. We quickly planned a memorial service to be held in our congregation where the entire local Jewish community could attend and show their support for her family.

The circumstances of the death were horrifying to say the least. The young woman had been at a shopping mall with her friend. They were about to complete their purchases in a store when the young lady started getting a feeling that something terrible was about to happen. This increased and in a panic she ran from the store to leave the mall and get to her car. Just as she approached the glass doors of the mall exit, with her friend chasing after her and calling to her, the terrorist stepped into the mall and blew himself up. The fireball and shrapnel killed her instantly and wounded her friend.

The victim's aunt asked me why would God have given her a message or feeling that this was about to happen? Had she not had the feeling but stayed in the store for a few more minutes she would not have been killed. Had she not rushed directly toward the terrorist she might have been only wounded at worst. Why would God do this? There is no good answer to this question. If I knew the Mind of God, I would be God. There are some questions for which no good answers exist, at least not while we live. The grief and horrible questions this murder raised made this the most difficult memorial service at which I have ever officiated.

Perhaps the most joyous moment in my rabbinic work was when I watched a community of strangers come together to make a dying Jewish woman's wish come true.

Our good friend Christine Goldman, who works with Jewish Family Services, had called asking if I could visit a woman on hospice care in Long Beach, CA. Chris is a close friend and was the maid of honor at our wedding. Chris' son Christopher was a junior Groomsman and looked dashing in his top hat. At the time I am writing this he is about to complete his Army Basic training! How fast time flies. When Chris met her husband to be, Paul Goldman, through JDate, my mother sat with Paul and assured him that Chris was a keeper. I had the honor of officiating at their wedding.

The critically ill woman that Chris knew was unaffiliated with a synagogue and had only her daughter to care for her. The doctors were very pessimistic about her odds of survival more than a few days.

Her name was Sylvia and she had a lovely and kind personality. We talked for a long time about her life, her love for her daughter Rebecca and for another daughter who had serious health challenges of her own. This was in late October 2013.

I mentioned to Sylvia that Chanukah was arriving early this year, falling on the same day as Thanksgiving. In fact this would be a once in a thousand lifetimes event as the two holidays would not coincide again for over 70,000 years. We were calling it 'Thanksgivukkah' and Jews were finding creative ways to observe both holidays at once.

A turkey menorah, called a '*Menurkey*' with the candles placed in its ceramic tail feathers was selling like hotcakes on the internet. Recipes such as potato latkes topped with fresh cranberry orange relish sounded yummy. Sylvia told me how much she loved Chanukah and was distressed that her doctors did not believe she would live to see this one.

If there is one thing I know about the Jewish Community, it is that we will rush to come to the assistance of a person in need, regardless of whether we know them personally. I put the word out to my congregants and colleagues that we needed to organize an early Chanukah celebration immediately to make Sylvia's wish come true. Chris rallied the troops at JFS as well.

People responded! The Hughes family and other Jews in Long Beach, My El Segundo congregant Jason Gertler, Jews from Torrance and Orange County started making holiday foods. A lady who played guitar and could sing agreed to lead some Chanukah songs. We invited all of the residents at the nursing home to attend.

On a glorious Sunday evening, a month before Chanukah officially started, Chanukah came to the nursing home. We lit the candles, sang songs, ate holiday treats such as potato latkes and jelly donuts and showered Sylvia with hugs and kisses.

Many people also scheduled time so that they could visit her during the following days. Sylvia got such a lift to her spirit! She ended up living several weeks beyond her doctor's expectations. I have never been so proud to be Jewish and living with such a wonderful community as on that day. Sylvia's funeral was well attended, with some of her new friends there.

Chapter 29 - What Does Judaism Say About Various Issues?

As a Rabbi, there are certain questions I am asked about frequently that I would like to touch upon. There is an old joke that a priest and a rabbi were debating about when life begins. The priest said life begins at the moment of conception. The Rabbi thought about it and said Jewish parents don't know if their child has a viable life until the kid graduates from medical or law school!

What does Judaism actually say about abortion? In Judaism there is a broad spectrum of observance. From the Hasidim and Orthodox who follow the traditions very strictly, through Conservative, Reform and Reconstructionist Judaism, there are many opinions on various topics. Abortion though tends be looked upon the same way by virtually all Jewish movements.

God told us to 'be fruitful and multiply' and raising children to be good, decent people, is one of the most important things a person can accomplish. Note that sex between married couples does not have to be for procreation but merely for giving pleasure to each other. Indeed, Jewish wives have the absolute right to demand or refuse sex from their husbands. Jewish law even states how often a wife should require sexual relations depending on whether her husband works close to home or is a sailor only home every six months. Using contraception to prevent pregnancy is not a problem. Abortion is not contraception and should not be thought of in that way.

Family means everything to Jews. Abortion is not a thing that should be done *unless necessary to save the life of the mother.*

Unlike Catholicism, where life is thought to begin at the moment of conception, in Judaism the baby is not considered viable until it can survive outside of the mother's body. If, God forbid, the baby dies within the first 30 days of birth, Jews traditionally do not observe all of the mourning customs one would do for a child's passing who had survived longer than a month.

The mother, an existing life, needs to have her life preserved above that of a potential life. Not all mothers with risky pregnancies will choose to have a medically necessary abortion. Jewish tradition though is clear on that point. Abortion is never to be thought of as 'emergency contraception' or a 'convenience.' Carrying and delivering the child and placing it for adoption is the far more praiseworthy and compassionate option.

So many couples cannot have children biologically and are waiting and dreaming to give loving homes to children in need. On matters of life and death I do believe God decides who is to be born and who is to die. Embrace life always.

Is sex outside of marriage allowed? This is a more challenging question than the abortion question. The ideal is to have sexual relations between consenting adults within marriage. Until a couple commits to each other completely and includes God in their wedding vows, they should not be engaging in sexual intercourse. Is it a sin for two consenting adults (neither of whom is married to someone else!) to have sex? It certainly isn't a sin like theft or murder, but it also isn't a *mitzvah*. (A Mitzvah is a commandment and praiseworthy deed) Biblically we even see a number of examples of prostitution being an accepted part of ancient society. Multiple wives were common until Rabbenu Gershom 1000 years ago decreed only one wife for one husband at a time.

God made us sexual creatures with innate needs and desires. We are told to control those needs and emotions to elevate us from the animals. Forcing sex through rape or coercion, or with an underage person, is absolutely a grave sin, and no always means no. Two consenting adult lovers giving pleasure to each other is not a terrible thing. Adultery is specifically forbidden in the Ten Commandments and is a serious matter to commit.

What about Same Sex Relations and Marriages? This is where different forms of Judaism vary widely from each other. The Orthodox and Hasidim will never recognize this as it is specifically prohibited in the Torah in the Book of Leviticus. Traditional congregations actually read these prohibitions aloud as part of the Yom Kippur Day afternoon service.

All other movements in Judaism are either tolerant or welcoming. There are reform and conservative openly gay and lesbian rabbis, cantors and even synagogues specifically welcoming to LGBT individuals and couples.

I follow the teaching of my ordaining Rabbi, Rabbi Joseph H. Gelberman, of blessed memory. He taught that we are all made in the image of God. Therefore no person could possibly be an 'abomination' based on how we are created. Being lesbian, gay, bisexual or transgender is not a choice for mot people. We are who we are and love whom we love. As a Rabbi it is not my place to reject anyone from having a close relationship with God and others.

I cheerfully officiate at same sex weddings. I don't believe in being *'tolerant'*. Tolerance simply means you are not actively rejecting someone. Who wants to just be tolerated? Instead, be welcoming to all and inclusive. Those against 'marriage equality' say it degrades their heterosexual marriage for LGBT couples to marry.

<u>The only thing that can affect a heterosexual marriage is the way the husband and wife treat each other.</u> External matters have little impact if the marriage is strong. We should support monogamous relationships and marriages between any two consenting adults as a societal good.

I think same sex couples should be able to adopt or raise children as they wish. Good parents raise upstanding children. Studies have not shown that the children of gay parents are any more likely to be gay or straight than the children of heterosexual couples. It is not a choice but genetics. Whatever goes on in the bedroom between the parents is not something children should be aware of or concerned with, no matter the makeup of their family.

What is the Jewish opinion on divorce? While the goal is for married couples to grow old with each other in love and joy, the reality is sometimes different. If a couple has differences they simply cannot overcome, divorce may be the best option.

The wording about divorce is crucial in the *ketubah*, the wedding contract, signed by the bride and groom. An orthodox text ketubah only gives the husband the right to pursue or disallow a divorce. Historically there have been terrible abuses because of this.

Imagine a bad husband who cheats on his wife or is violent to her and the children. The wife cannot force a divorce without his consent. In ancient times this was perhaps less of a problem in that the Rabbis would haul the husband into a *Beit Din*, a Jewish court, and demand that he grant a divorce. If he refused, the Rabbis would have some big fellows beat on him to sign off on it. If he still refused, they would beat him to death and then she was free to remarry as a widow. If only we modern Rabbis had this authority!

The conservative and Reform movements have a solution to this, called the *Lieberman* clause. It gives equal rights to both spouses to terminate the marriage. I will not officiate at a wedding unless the ketubah uses this language or the couple has a very good reason to use the traditional language.

To get divorced, a Rabbi or scribe will draw up a personalized Aramaic bill of divorce document known as a *'Get.'* This document is 12 lines long and signed by witnesses beneath the 12th line in the presence of a *Beit Din*, rabbinic court.

About 1000 years ago a German Jewish sage named Rabbenu Gershom stated that both parties must agree to the Get for it to be valid. His ruling governs *Ashkenazic* European Jews.

Sephardic Judaism had different requirements up until quite recently. The party wanting the divorce, traditionally the husband, will hand it to the other spouse. This is done in front of a rabbinic court whose judges are experts in the matter. Each Get is individually crafted for the couple, there are no form Gets. They should also comply with Civil divorce laws and procedures. Note though that a civil divorce filed with the state does not accomplish a Jewish divorce in the eyes of a rabbinic court.

No matter how long the couple are separated from each other, only the preparation, signing by witnesses and handing over of the Get accomplishes the actual Jewish divorce. Usually money or spousal support is also exchanged, particularly if one spouse does not have independent income. Traditionally the wife must take the Get and walk a little distance holding it as a sign of owning it. The Get will then be cut so it cannot be used again and it is stored away. The Beit Din will order the divorced couple not to live together and to avoid being alone with each other if possible. Should they end up wishing to remarry each other, that is permissible and often encouraged.

When a spouse goes missing, such as during a war or disaster, and is not heard from by the other spouse, they will eventually be declared dead so the surviving spouse can remarry. A rabbinic court can issue a *Heter Agunah* ruling, freeing the spouse to remarry, although it is a very complex process under Jewish law. Witnesses will be questioned and generally a waiting period of years must be completed.

Upon death, is cremation allowed? Traditionally, Jews have overwhelmingly always favored ground burials going back to when Abraham bought a burial plot and used it to bury his wife Sarah. It is thought to be the best way in Jewish law to fulfill the Biblical requirement of honoring the dead in a respectful way. One is not allowed to mutilate a corpse. Burial leads to natural decomposition, *'from dust to dust,'* whereas cremation is an instant destruction of the corpse akin to mutilation by Jewish tradition. Jews don't embalm bodies generally so as to allow decomposition to occur naturally.

When our Torah scrolls are damaged to where they cannot be repaired, we are obligated to give them a ground burial as opposed to burning them. Cremation was known in ancient times and was considered a pagan ritual.

Many orthodox Rabbis and some Conservative Rabbis will not officiate at a service with cremated remains although most Jewish cemeteries allow the practice. My personal practice is to advise families about the tradition and let them decide. In particular, after millions of Jews were murdered and burned during the Holocaust, I find the idea of burning a corpse to be repugnant. Fifteen years ago only a very tiny fraction of Jews chose cremation, less than 2%. Today in 2014 the rate may be as high as 10 or 11% in some areas.

Can Jews get tattoos? The Torah commands us not to make marks or cuts upon our body and tattoos are included in that prohibition. The body is a gift from God and other than male circumcision or surgical procedures for health we should not permanently alter our body's appearance.

Where a tattoo is needed for medical reasons, such as a focal point for radiation therapy there is no issue whatsoever. Virtually any of the 613 commandments other than killing an innocent person may be transgressed for medical or life saving reasons. I have read and agree with some rabbinic *responsa* that allows a tattoo to cover up a bad scar if the disfiguring scar is preventing the person from enjoying their life. As far as I know, Jewish cemeteries in the USA do not refuse to bury Jewish people with tattoos.

When a tattoo is done against a person's will, such as a concentration camp number during the Holocaust, there is absolutely no issue at all. Some orthodox burial societies call such a number 'a passport.' This means that the person has already survived hell during life and the tattoo is a direct passport into heaven without delay.

Is Organ Donation allowed? Organ donation after death to help heal or save another life is a meritorious thing to do and should be encouraged. Making a donation of a kidney during life is more of a challenge from a Jewish legal standpoint.

If it can be done without undue risk to the donor's life, it should be permissible to save the life of another. If the surgery puts the donor in an immediate life threatening situation it should not be done, as again the rule is to preserve existing life over potential life. A comatose patient should not be taken off life support and have organs harvested if there is a chance of awakening and recovery. If a person can move even one finger there is hope of living a worthwhile life, says our Tradition. Where there is no possibility of recovery, such as in actual brain death, it is better to let the body be at peace and to save lives with the organs if possible.

Did the Jews kill Jesus? Why don't the Jews Accept Jesus as the Messiah?

Without question, Jews believe that Jesus lived and was a known 1st Century Rabbi. He is quoted in the Talmud as *'Rav Yeshua D'Nazareth'* taking part in a discussion on Passover observance. The accounts in the gospels, particularly in the Gospel of Matthew, of his statements to love others, reflect many ideas held by other contemporaneous Rabbis including Rabbi Hillel and Rabbi Akiba.

I read recently Bill O'Reilly and Martin Dugard's book KILLING JESUS and found it to be a fact based excellent book describing the interaction between the Jews and the Roman Empire during that time period. I recommend it to all looking to understand the politics and established facts on the subject. By all accounts the execution of Jesus was a brutal and torturous Roman method by crucifixion. Thousand of Jews and Rabbis died horrible deaths on Roman crosses.

The execution was carried out by Roman soldiers, not by Jews. Crucifixion was not a method used by Jews to execute criminals.

We do not have independent Jewish texts describing a conflict between Jesus and the High Priest Caiaphous or the Sanhedrin. We also don't have texts describing his resurrection or a virgin birth.

Jews reject the idea that the Messiah has come because the Torah describes a lasting time of peace when all nations shall serve God. Our world is every bit as violent and brutal today as it was 2000 years ago. We do believe that the Messiah *will* come, when all turn away from senseless violence and hatred and respect God and spirituality in all humans.

CHAPTER 30 - DO JEWS BELIEVE IN AN "END TIMES" SCENARIO?

We do, but not like the Christian belief in the rapture, tribulation, antichrist and second coming of Jesus. The Jewish belief is that the Jews that have been dispersed throughout all of the countries will be gathered together again in Israel. The Temple will be rebuilt on the Temple Mount (where the Dome of the Rock mosque presently sits) and a direct descendant of King David through King Solomon will be anointed the Messiah. He will be fully human and not divine. This individual will bring about an enduring and lasting peace to the world where all will recognize the God of Israel. Historically there was belief in the physical resurrection of the dead and the very righteous of all peoples. There was a belief that death will cease and predatory animals will become vegetarians and live in peace with what would have been their prey.

Maimonides, the famed Spanish Rabbi and Scholar, wrote the following more understandable description in his commentary on the Mishnah, tractate Sanhedrin 10:1

"The Messianic age is when the Jews will regain their independence and all return to the land of Israel. The Messiah will be a very great king, he will achieve great fame, and his reputation among the gentile nations will be even greater than that of King Solomon. His great righteousness and the wonders that he will bring about will cause all peoples to make peace with him and all lands to serve him.... Nothing will change in the Messianic age, however, except that Jews will regain their independence. Rich and poor, strong and weak, will still exist. However it will be very easy for people to make a living, and with very little effort they will be able to accomplish very much.... it will be a time when the number of wise men will increase.... war shall not exist, and nation shall no longer lift up sword against nation.... The Messianic age will be highlighted by a community of the righteous and dominated by goodness and wisdom. It will be ruled by the Messiah, a righteous and honest king, outstanding in wisdom, and close to God. Do not think that the ways of the world or the laws of nature will change, this is not true. The world will continue as it is. The

prophet Isaiah predicted "The wolf shall live with the sheep; the leopard shall lie down with the kid." This, however, is merely allegory, meaning that the Jews will live safely, even with the formerly wicked nations. All nations will return to the true religion and will no longer steal or oppress. Note that all prophecies regarding the Messiah are allegorical. Only in the Messianic age will we know the meaning of each allegory and what it comes to teach us. Our sages and prophets did not long for the Messianic age in order that they might rule the world and dominate the gentiles, the only thing they wanted was to be free for Jews to involve themselves with the Torah and its wisdom"

CHAPTER 31 - WHAT IS THE JEWISH CALENDAR AND WHY ARE MONDAYS SO DIFFICULT?

Jews follow a lunar calendar rather than the more accurate solar calendar. Each month is around 28 days long. Days begin at sunset and end the following sunset. The new month starts when there is verification by sight of the very thinnest crescent of moon at sunset following the new moon. The reason we start days at sunset is based on the Creation story in Genesis where each day of Creation started at sunset. Leap years with an extra month of Adar are added frequently so that the holidays stay within a month or so of the secular calendar each year. Most Rabbis do not know when the coming year's holidays will fall without consulting a Jewish calendar. These are often given away for free by Jewish Mortuaries, and many synagogues hand them out in the Fall during the High Holy Day services. You can also access the Jewish calendar at the website www.Hebcal.com which will convert secular dates and events into Hebrew dates and vice versa.

Did you ever wonder why Mondays tend to be so miserable? True, we enjoy our weekends, but Mondays are often particularly challenging. I place the blame on God. On all of the days of Creation God pronounced the day as Good or even Very Good. God doesn't say a thing about Monday though, where there was no real 'creation' but rather a separation of the waters above from those below. If God found being Creative on Monday challenging, we shouldn't beat ourselves up if we find the day difficult as well!

Virtually every month of the year contains a Jewish holiday, festival or observance. This gives a rhythmic flow to our lives and makes each part of the year meaningful.

On a weekly basis, the Sabbath, which Jews call *Shabbat* in Hebrew, gives us a day of complete rest. In ancient times this was unheard of. People worked long hours seven days per week.

God rested on the 7th day of creation and decreed that we should take a day of complete rest as well, including our working animals, servants and any non-Jews living amongst us. Shabbat is a day of prayer, song, special meals, attending services, spending time with family and friends and of study.

Traditional Jews do not drive cars, turn on and off lights or do a myriad of other tasks deemed to be work from Sundown Friday until Sundown Saturday.

Just as the 7th day is holy, so too the 7th month called *'Tishrei'* which arrives in the Fall, is very sacred. Preparations for the month of Tishrei start in the 6th month, called *Elul*. Tradition tells us that Elul is an acronym in Hebrew for *'Ani L'Dodi V'Dodi Li' 'I am my beloved's and my beloved is mine.'* As the Summer draws to a close and Fall begins we are to take stock of ourselves. Are we satisfied with our lives or can we make changes to better ourselves and our family and community?

Special prayers of repentence, called *'Selichot,'* are recited starting in Elul and many congregations start sounding the ram's horn, the *shofar*, as a reminder that the New Year, *Rosh Hashana*, and Day of Atonement, *Yom Kippur* are fast approaching. Why a Ram's Horn? It is because when Abraham was prepared to sacrifice Isaac, God stopped him and had him take a ram that caught by its horns in a thicket as a substitute sacrifice.

While we appeal to God to be merciful on us, the warbling sound of the shofar reminds God of Abraham's sacrifice and maybe some of his merit can be used to spare each of us as well. This period is known as the High Holy Days. On the Saturday night before Rosh Hashana, special late night Selichot prayers are said and most congregations dress the Torah scrolls in white for the holidays.

The arrival of Rosh Hashana is not greeted with drunken partying like the secular New Year. It is a joyous yet somber day. This day is also called "*Yom Ha Din*" "The Day of Judgment". It is said to be the anniversary of the creation of the World. Each year on this day, God judges all of creation for the year to come. Have animals done what they were supposed to do in the prior year? Did trees and plants yield their fruit and flowers? Have humans done acts of kindness and compassion?

If we know we are lacking in any area, we use the ten days between Rosh Hashana and Yom Kippur to make changes. The shofar is sounded 100 times on Rosh Hashana Day, unless it coincides with Shabbat. The liturgy has special mournful melodies and the services are very long. We eat apple slices dipped in honey as a symbol of our wishes to be blessed with a sweet and good year. The *Tashlikh* service of casting crumbs into a body of water, described earlier in the book, is done on the afternoon of the first day of Rosh Hashana, unless it coincides with Shabbat. Rosh Hashana used to be the first day of the First month, when the calendar year flipped over. It is an ancient holiday that existed before the Exodus as a day to 'coronate' God as our King each year.

The Exodus and Passover though was such an important event, in the Spring time month of *Nisan* (around April) that Nisan was renamed the first month of the year. This led to the weird situation where the calendar year flips over in the 7th month of Tishrei, but the months are numbered from Nisan onward.

Rosh Hashana lasts for two days outside of Israel, partly due to the uncertainty of when the new month of Tishrei arrives since a visual sighting of the new thinnest crescent of the moon is used to establish the date.

Yom Kippur is the holiest day of the Jewish calendar. A twenty four hour complete fast from all drinking and eating starts at sundown on Yom Kippur Eve. Anyone healthy enough to abstain from all food and water who is over age 13 is expected to fast. Generally families eat a large meal prior to the start of the day.

We go to synagogue on Yom Kippur Eve where a special Aramaic piece of liturgy called *Kol Nidrei* is sung. In past ages Jews were forced to convert to be spared from being murdered. Entire communities were being martyred rather than convert. The Rabbis decreed that Jews should say or do anything short of killing another person to stop the slaughter.

On this holiest day of the year we ask God to absolve us from forced vows and actions, and from acts we promised and intended to do, but could not do. So important is this recitation that many people refer to the Eve of Yom Kippur as *Erev Kol Nidrei – The Evening of Kol Nidrei.* It is the one night of the year when Jewish people wear their prayer shawls at night.

The next day is full of daylong services until sunset. We read several times from the Torah scroll and make five group confessionals. We read what is essentially a funeral liturgy and are asked to visualize ourselves as dying. We are begging for forgiveness from God and must ask forgiveness from those we have wronged. Prayers emphasizing the frailty of life and God's Eternity are read and sung. We dress in white, most traditionally in a burial shroud called a "*kittel*". In Middle Eastern cultures, white is not just a symbol of purity but of death. We strip away the masks we wear and really take a hard look at ourselves.

The central prayer is the *Untane Tokef.* It is said that the 11th Century sage, Rabbi Amnon of Mainz, Germany composed it on his death as a martyr. Rabbi Amnom was a friend of the Archbishop of Mainz. They had theological disputes and discussions. Once the Archbishop asked Rabbi Amnom to consider converting to Roman Catholicism. Instead of declining immediately he asked for three days to consider the matter and then would return to give his answer. He immediately regretted that decision as nothing could persuade him to convert from Judaism. He failed to return on the third day and was seized and brought before the Archbishop. The Archbishop wished to punish him for failing to return as he had promised and for not converting. Rabbi Amnom suggested that his tongue be cut from his mouth because he did not live up to his promise to return. The Archbishop refused this and ordered that each hand and leg be cut off, one at a time. After each amputation he was asked to convert but refused. While dying, on Rosh Hashana day, he asked to be carried into the synagogue where he made the following proclamation which is now a part of the standard liturgy:

We shall ascribe holiness to this day.

For it is awesome and terrible.

Your kingship is exalted upon it.

Your throne is established in mercy.

You are enthroned upon it in truth.

In truth You are the judge,

The exhorter, the all knowing, the witness,

He who inscribes and seals,

Remembering all that is forgotten.

You open the book of remembrance

Which proclaims itself,

And the seal of each person is there.

The great shofar is sounded,

A still small voice is heard.

The angels are dismayed,

They are seized by fear and trembling

As they proclaim: Behold the Day of Judgment!

For all the hosts of heaven are brought for judgment.

They shall not be guiltless in Your eyes

And all creatures shall parade before You as a troop.

As a shepherd herds his flock,

Causing his sheep to pass beneath his staff,

So do You cause to pass, count, and record,

Visiting the souls of all living,

Decreeing the length of their days,

Inscribing their judgment.

On Rosh Hashanah it is inscribed,

And on Yom Kippur it is sealed.

How many shall pass away and how many shall be born,

Who shall live and who shall die,

Who shall reach the end of his days and who shall not,

Who shall perish by water and who by fire,

Who by sword and who by wild beast,

Who by famine and who by thirst,

Who by earthquake and who by plague,

Who by strangulation and who by stoning,

Who shall have rest and who shall wander,

Who shall be at peace and who shall be pursued,

Who shall be at rest and who shall be tormented,

Who shall be exalted and who shall be brought low,

Who shall become rich and who shall be impoverished.

But repentance, prayer and righteousness avert the severe decree.

For Your praise is in accordance with Your name. You are difficult to anger and easy to appease. For You do not desire the death of the condemned, but that he turn from his path and live. Until the day of his death You wait for him. Should he turn, You will receive him at once. In truth You are their Creator and You understand their inclination, for they are but flesh and blood. The origin of man is dust, his end is dust. He earns his bread by exertion and is like a broken shard, like dry grass, a withered flower, like a passing shadow and a vanishing cloud, like a breeze that blows away and dust that scatters, like a dream that flies away. But You are King, God who lives for all eternity! There is no limit to Your years, no end to the length of Your days, no measure to the hosts of Your glory, no understanding the meaning of Your Name. Your Name is fitting unto You and You are fitting unto it, and our name has been called by Your Name. Act for the sake of Your Name and sanctify Your Name through those who sanctity Your Name.

Rabbi Alan Lew wrote a wonderful book about the High Holy Days called 'THIS IS REAL AND YOU ARE COMPLETELY UNPREPARED.' that I recommend highly. Rabbi Lew correctly points out that living a righteous life does not prevent tragedy and sorrow, but it transforms the nature of those bad things. Instead of viewing them as punishments, our faith allows us to survive these events and grow spiritually. Growing up I must have been a weird kid, because my favorite holiday was and remains Yom Kippur. It speaks of the harsh reality of death and pushes us to make the most of each day we are granted.

The High Holy Days then continues with the holidays of *Sukkot* and *Simchat Torah*. During *Sukkot* Jews build *sukkah* booths with palm fronds for thatch. We can see the stars through the fronds at night and the wind and rain is free to enter. The booths are decorated and we symbolically invite the Patriarchs and Matriarchs to join us in the sukkah. Jews eat their meals and some sleep in the sukkah for a week.

This reminds us and God of the desert booths the Jews lived in for forty years after leaving Egypt.

We take four species of plants together and shake them in all directions while singing Psalms. They are the *lulav*, which is the spine of the palm frond, the *etrog* – a lemony smelling citron which dries up but doesn't rot, and leaves of myrtle and willow trees. We hold these together symbolizing our bodies. The lulav represents our backs which should be upright in serving God. The myrtle represents our eyes, which should look for opportunities to do God's Will. The willow represents our lips, which should be used to utter praise to God and to speak kind and truthful words. The *etrog* represents our heart which should be dedicated to serving God.

It also represents the four types of people, all of whom serve God together as the House of Israel and really represent all people. The palm spine itself has no smell but yields tasty dates. This represents a person with no Torah learning of their own to speak of, but who does good deeds or raises good children that have a positive impact on the world.

The myrtle has a pleasant smell but no taste. This is like someone who studies Torah but does not do good deeds as a result.

The willow has neither smell nor taste and represents those who don't study Torah and who don't do good deeds.

Finally the etrog has both a pleasant smell and lemony taste, representing those who both study Torah and do good deeds. Without the willow one hasn't performed the *mitzvah*, the commandment, to hold and use the Four Species together in praise of God.

On *Yom Kippur* and on *Sukkot, Shavuot and Passover*, we have a special service called the *Yizkor*, memorial service where we remember the lives of our parents, close relatives and friends who have passed away. We also remember the victims of the Holocaust and other martyrs who may not have anyone alive to remember them. We pledge charity in their names and are reminded of the good examples they set for us to follow.

The High Holidays ends with Simchat Torah, literally "Rejoicing of the Torah" where we eat and imbibe to feel joyful as we complete the yearly Torah reading cycle and start anew. We read the last lines of Deuteronomy talking about the death of Moses, and immediately read the first lines of the Creation story in Genesis. We dance with the Torah scrolls and are thankful for the life we are given.

Around November or December, on the 25th day of the Hebrew month of Kislev, we celebrate the Festival of Lights, *Chanukah.*

I find Chanukah and *Purim* in the Spring to be the easiest holidays to relate to. In each case we read about how God surreptitiously, behind the scenes, saved the Jewish Community.

The Jews in the Chanukah story decided to fight oppression without the aid of a prophet or other assurance that God was with them. There were no visible miracles as during the Exodus and no Voice of God from the heavens guiding them. They were ordinary people who risked their lives for their faith and for religious freedom.

In the Chanukah story, in 168 B.C.E. the Assyrian Greeks tried to force the Jews to worship Emperor Antiochus Epiphanes and Zeus. Many refused and were publicly and brutally slaughtered. Antiochus ordered that pigs be sacrificed in the Temple in Jerusalem and that other pagan rites be done which rendered the place unusable for Jewish worship.

In the town of Modiin, which still exists in modern Israel, an elderly man called Matathias had enough and together with his sons killed the soldiers and started a war. One son in particular, Judah, was a powerful warrior who gathered an army of Jews to confront the Assyrian Greek military, the most powerful in the world at that time. The rebels called themselves Maccabees. This might be a derivative of the Hebrew word for hammer, *Makav*, referring to their hard hitting warfare style. Or it could be a reference to the Biblical song sung at the Red Sea when God killed the Egyptian pursuers in the sea. The people sang '*Mi Khamokha Ba'elim Adonai – Who is Like You Among the gods that are worshipped?*' The acronym for the Hebrew phrase is Maccabee and they might have wanted a connection to ancient Israel's most dramatic salvation by God at the Red Sea.

Through guerilla warfare tactics they eventually drove the Greeks from the land and rededicated the Temple. It took eight days to rededicate it, following the pattern of the 8 day dedication of the wilderness tabernacle by Moses and Aaron, and the eight day dedication by King Solomon of the First Temple in Jerusalem.

It is said that only one jar of pure olive oil bearing the undisturbed seal of the High Priest could be found and it would take a week to make more. The great *Menorah* of the Temple mount, a huge seven branched lamp, burned gallons of olive oil per day. It was to be kept lit at all times. The light was so bright when it was lit in the courtyard of the Temple Mount in Jerusalem that it could be seen from 20 miles away.

The Rabbis decided not to wait a week but to light it immediately. Our job is to bring light to the world and banish spiritual darkness. A miracle happened where the oil burned for eight days until a new batch could be prepared.

We celebrate the holiday for eight nights. We follow the directions of Rabbi Hillel, to add a candle each night until we have a fully lit *Chanukiah*, Chanukah menorah, on the eighth night.

Traditionally we play a game with the *dreidle* top. It has four letters on its sides representing *'Nes Gadol Haya Sham'* *'A great miracle happened there.'*

This top had a historical role as well. While planning the war, **Jewish** soldiers would meet in public places spinning a dreidle, called a *Sevivon* in Hebrew, to make it look like they were gambling instead of discussing an attack. Chocolate 'Gelt' coins are also given out to represent that the Maccabees won the right to mint their own coinage without the hated image of Antiochus on it.

Jelly donuts, called *sufganiyot,* and Potato pancakes, called *Latkes,* are served during the holiday. Foods fried in Olive Oil remind us of the miracle of the oil and are yummy if not exactly healthy.

Purim, which arrives around March each year in the month of *Adar*, is based on the Biblical scroll/Book of Esther. It describes how a Jewish girl named Hadassah, took the Persian name Esther and was selected to be the wife of King Achashveyrosh of Persia. This King is also known as Xerxes the Great who lived around 500 B.C.E. She hid her Jewish identity from the King.

The King's Prime Minister, Haman, said to be a descendant of the ancient Amalakites, who committed senseless slaughter on the Jews during the Exodus, rose to power. He cast lots called "*Purim*" in Hebrew and picked a date of the 14th of Adar for the slaughter of all Jews in Persia. He convinced the King to sign the order saying that the Jews were not loyal to him but worshipped their own God. Haman was angry that the Jews did not bow down to him, who had the image of his pagan god on his chest. He told the King that his soldiers would take all Jewish valuables and land and give it to the King's treasury.

Without word from God, Esther consulted her cousin Mordechai, who was a Jewish sage. He told her she must speak to the King to save the community. She was afraid because the King would kill her if she entered to see him uninvited. Mordechai uttered the famous line 'Perhaps it was for just such a time as this that you were chosen to become the Queen.' (Esther 4:14) She could either do her job for her community or be killed with them. God would find another way to accomplish His Will if she refused.

It is fascinating book. Everything Haman does backfires on him. **Mordechai** is raised to prominence for uncovering a plot to kill the King and Haman is ordered personally to dress him in royal clothes and lead him around publicly on a horse saying 'Thus is done to honor the man the King wishes to honor.' Queen Esther hosts a number of banquets to which she invites Haman and the King. At the last banquet she asks the King to spare her life and the life of her people from Haman's evil decree. In shock the King leaves the room and Haman throws himself down before the Queen on her sofa to beg for his life. The King sees this and accuses Haman of trying to rape the Queen! Before he can say a word he is hauled off and hanged on a 70 foot high gallows he had built to hang Mordechai upon. His ten sons and evil wife Zeresh were hanged as well.

The King granted the Jews the right to defend themselves and they won the battles of the day. Forever after the Rabbis declared this to be a holiday of joy. People get drunk to the point that they can't understand the difference between 'bless Mordechai and curse Haman.' Gifts of food are sent to the Poor and to friends as well. Children and lots of adults dress up in costumes and do special songs and comedy skits at a service where the Book of Esther is publicly read. We boo and use noisemakers called *groggers*, to drown out the name of Haman whenever it is read. We eat Hamentaschen, a cookie dough pastry filled with jam or poppy seeds shaped like the three pointed hat Haman supposedly wore.

Interestingly, this holiday falls virtually six months to the day after Yom Kippur. Yom Kippur is also known *Yom Ha Kippurim*, which means either the "*Day of Atonements*" or "the *Day which is Like Purim.*" They are exact opposites half a year apart. Yom Kippur is a deadly serious day of fasting where we strip off the masks we hide ourselves behind and acknowledge what God knows, our true selves. Purim is anything but serious. We dress in costumes and hide our real selves, symbolizing how God worked hidden behind the scenes. We eat and drink with abandon. These days balance each other out.

The next really major Festival is Passover in the Spring time around April. Passover is a very important festival, arguably the most important of the three Pilgrimage festivals In ancient Israel, Jews would travel to the Temple in Jerusalem to sacrifice and celebrate. Modernly families and friends gather on the first two nights of the weeklong holiday and retell the story of the Exodus while eating ceremonial foods at a *Seder* dinner. Prior to that the house is scrubbed clean of any trace of bread or leavened items.

Curiously, when the 'Black Death' Bubonic plague swept through Medievel Europe killing millions, Jews were not infected and dying as much as their gentile neighbors. Scholars believe the yearly cleaning for any crumbs kept the mice and rats out of Jewish homes. The rodents went to homes with bread crumbs on the floors and their fleas transmitted the plague.

Special plates and bowls for Passover are used that have never had bread on them. A Seder booklet called the *Hagaddah* tells the story in Hebrew, Aramaic and the vernacular language of each country. All in attendance participate in the Seder. The youngest child able to read asks the Four Questions and four glasses of wine are consumed during the Seder.

As a reminder that the Jews who left Egypt departed in such a hurry that their bread didn't have time to rise before being baked, we eat Matzo crackers in place of bread products for the week. Consisting of wheat flour mixed with water and baked at a high temperature matzo is thin and crispy.

Products containing yeast or any leavening agent are not allowed during the holiday. Sephardic Jews will eat rice and corn whereas traditional Ashkenazic Jews won't. The reason they won't is that they could be ground up and mistaken for wheat flour that has not been guarded against exposure to yeast. Matzo is ceremonially eaten during the Seder with bitter herbs. We also eat parsley dipped in salt water, *charoset* – a chopped apple, nuts, cinammon and sweet wine mixture resembling the mortar the Jewish slaves used to build the cities of Pithom and Raamses for Pharoah. An egg representing the Spring is present along with a roasted lamb shank bone recalling the ancient Passover offering. It tends to be a fun holiday surrounded by family and friends and synagogue services.

On the fiftieth day after Passover Jews welcome the Festival of *Shavuot* (usually around June). This holiday celebrates the gift of the Torah and the Ten Commandments. It recalls the Revelation at Mount Sinai on the 50th day after the Exodus from Egypt. Every man, woman and child assembled at the foot of the mountain heard the Voice of God and saw the mountain burning with fire and smoke like a furnace. Thunder and lightning boomed. The earth was quaking and an unseen heavenly Shofar sounded, walking through the camp getting louder and louder.

It was overwhelming and terrifying. Each of the people then heard the Ten Commandments uttered at the same time. Some heard it as quiet as a whisper, others heard it at a loud volume, in whatever way the individual would respond best. There is a tradition to eat dairy dishes on this holiday and to publicly read the Ten Commandments from the Torah scroll.

Often conversions are done at this holiday as well as confirmation ceremonies for post bar and bat mitzvah students. It is said that if you study all night on Erev Shavuot and look to the heavens at midnight you might catch a glimpse of God's heavenly realm, The Book of Ruth is studied as well.

Other holidays are celebrated throughout the year as well.

On Tisha B'Av in late Summer, Jews observe a fast day and read from the Book of Lamentations. Historically it has been a terrible day for the Jews. Both Temples fell on the 9th of Av hundreds of years apart. The expulsion of the Jews from Spain in 1492, The Wansee Conference where the Holocaust was planned by the Nazis, even the final destruction of the Warsaw Ghetto during the Holocaust, all happened on the 9th of Av.

Why is this day such a bad one? Tradition says that when Moses sent the spies to spy on ancient Israel prior to their conquest of it, they returned on the 9th of Av with a bad report of the land and the people wailed for no reason. Because of this event, God decreed that the people will have actual reasons to mourn on that day until the Messianic Age arrives.

Other modern holidays include *Yom HaShoa* when we remember the victims of the Holocaust and *Yom Ha-Atz,m'ut* Israeli Independence Day.

On *Tu B'Shvat,* the Jewish Arbor Day, also known as the New Year for Trees, we celebrate trees and growing things. We plant trees and eat fruit. In ancient times this day was when the age of fruit trees was calculated for purposes of tithing.

On *Lag BaOmer*, the 33rd day of the Omer period between Passover and Shavuot, we read stories of Rabbi Shimon Bar Yohai, who passed away on this day after creating and reciting the Kabbalistic Book of Zohar to his disciples. Historically a terrible plague among yeshiva students in ancient Israel was ended on this day. There is a large gathering in Israel by Rabbi Shimon's grave.

Other customs include Jews practicing archery, and having a celebratory campfire or bonfire.

Finally the month of Elul arrives, usually in August or September, and the High Holy Day season starts anew.

Chapter 32 - Why do Jews Circumcise their males and what about conversion to Judaism?

As families and communities we gather together to celebrate the birth of children, baby namings, and a *bris* – circumcision ceremony for 8 day old boys, bar and bat mitzvahs, weddings and funerals. A Jewish life is very full of both joyous and sad times.

I want to say a word about circumcision as that is a hotly debated topic. The practice goes back to Abraham, the first Jew. God told Abraham to circumcise himself, his 13 year old son Ishmael, and all of the men in his camp. It is to be a sign of the covenant with God. He did so on the spot using flint knives.

Modernly, a specially trained doctor, called a Mohel, uses traditional steel surgical instruments to do the procedure quickly and professionally. Usually it is done at the family home, surrounded by relatives and friends. I always recommend a good Mohel over a general urologist in a hospital setting, where the procedure takes longer and the clamping involved is more distressing to the baby.

For Jews there is no option but to circumcise, as the boy won't be Jewish unless it is done. The removed foreskin is buried in soil after the procedure.

For males who convert to Judaism it is an absolute requirement that this be done. A convert who is already circumcised will have a drop of blood drawn from the head of the penis while the traditional blessings are recited. While there may be health benefits to those who are circumcised, it is done strictly for spiritual reasons and is not optional. There is no similar procedure for females.

If not required, some Jews probably would not choose to have the procedure done, but there is no choice for religious reasons. A parent who does not circumcise their son at 8 days is opening him up to a world of pain if later in life he chooses to become Orthodox or to marry a Jewish woman. Adult circumcisions are far more painful and dangerous to perform.

The question is asked 'Do Jews who have the procedure done lose sensitivity in the head of the penis?' While I have no basis of comparison, I can assure you that sex is pretty wonderful while circumcised. Even very old Jewish men still retain their sex drives. I do like to joke though that I had it done at age 8 days and couldn't walk afterwards for nearly a year!

Is there conversion to Judaism? Jews have never proselytized to convert others to Judaism. Rabbis will even discourage potential converts several times to make sure of their sincerity and reasons for conversion.

Looking at the billions of Christians and Muslims, Jews could have been the largest religion on earth had we actively tried to convert others over the millennia. We don't because it obligates the convert to observe the Commandments, not just the Ten famous ones, but hundreds of other Commandments.

Dietary laws, Shabbat laws, there are laws covering every aspect of life and death. For those not raised in a Jewish home it can seem overwhelming. We believe that we are individually responsible to God for our souls and life choices. There is no priest to absolve us, nor Savior to bear the load of our sins. We have to live an upright life and correct the wrongs we do.

Those who do choose to convert will study for many months to learn the customs and traditions. They will learn some Hebrew and attend services. Males will undergo circumcision or have a drop of blood drawn. They will present a certificate confirming this to the rabbinic court.

When the time is right the convert will renounce their former faith and be tested by a Beit Din, a rabbinic court, who will approve or reject their request. Generally the person is ready for conversion when they go before the Beit Din and rejection very rarely occurs. They will then be immersed in a ritual bath, a *Mikveh*, or they can immerse in the ocean, a river or a lake with running water. They recite the Shma prayer affirming their belief that God is One, and are then granted a Hebrew name.

They are given a certificate of conversion. Converts take the Hebrew names of Abraham and Sarah as their spiritual parents. For example, if a man chooses the name Yaakov (Jacob) for a Hebrew name, he will be called *Yaakov Ben Avraham v' Sarah*. From that moment onward the person is 100% Jewish. Converts may not be treated differently than those born to Jewish parents. Anyone who does so has committed a very grave sin.

Chapter 33 – Closing Thoughts And Why I Learned To Ride A Harley Davidson Motorcycle

What I would like to impart as the main message of my rabbinic calling is the following:

Life is very fleeting and fragile, so seize every day as a Divine gift and make the most of it. We never know how much time we have left. The past is behind us and cannot be changed, the future may not come though we plan for it, so all we definitely have to work with is today.

Tell people you love how you feel about them. How many were killed on September 11th who left their homes without saying goodbye or I love you to a spouse or children? How many parents sent their children off to Columbine or Newtown without saying "I love you" before a school day that turned to horror?

If a relationship with a spouse, child, relative, lover or friend is in disarray, the time to mend it is now. Do you have an elderly relative or neighbor you haven't spoken to in a while? Why not make a call or pay a visit. Something as easy as mailing a handwritten card or note can make their day.

Is there someone you know in the hospital or ill at home? Try making them my Mom's matzo ball soup and bring them some. I guarantee it will give them a lift and help them to feel better. Is there a book you want to read, a language you want to learn, a trip you want to take or an instrument you want to play? Go for it!

Is your career where you want it to be? Can you study a course, learn a new skill, or try something new to improve your current situation or to prepare for another career?

Do you need to lose some weight or is there a sport or activity you want to try? There is no time like the present. I think the hardest thing to do is to take the first step towards change. Once you start it gets easier, taking things one day at a time.

Never, ever hesitate to say a kind word or render a good deed. If a biting remark or negative comment or action wants to go forth, be careful what you say or do lest any harm result from it.

Take time for spirituality. Read about a variety of religions and beliefs. Debate and consider and ask questions, lots of questions. Attend a variety of services to find what calls to you. If you are born into a faith, truly explore it before casting it aside. Don't forget that we need spirituality like we need food and water. Don't deprive yourself of this necessity.

If you are aware of a social or community wrong that needs to be corrected, give of your time, effort or money to help correct it. Stand up for those whose rights are being trampled even if it is not the popular thing to do. Help those in need cheerfully for God will bless and repay you for your kindness and efforts on behalf of others.

Finally, live your life with a sense of faith and hope. There is a reason that you are you, born to live in this time and place. Know that while it is true that there are evil and bad people, most people are kind and good hearted. If you treat others with dignity, kindness and respect, most people will respond the same way. Avoid negative people where possible.

For years I had dreamed of riding a motorcycle. My parents made it clear that this was a dangerous thought that could lead to me being mangled or killed. I held off on pursuing this dream until the year 2000. I was sitting in a café next to a state office building in Santa Monica with my friend and opposing counsel Richard Mark Baker. We were trying to resolve a complex legal case involving an injured longshoreman. Suddenly the plate glass window exploded inwards and I was violently thrown from my chair into a small salad bar. I crashed to the tile floor fracturing my knee joint and herniating a back disc, both which I did not realize until several hours later.

I was covered in glass, on the floor, cursing my head off in a manner that would have made a 20 year Navy veteran proud. I thought a bomb had detonated at the courthouse next door. Mr. Baker, himself covered with shattered glass, helped me up and showed me what had happened.

A young (and uninsured) woman had driven her parent's Volvo through the restaurant. She hit the gas instead of the brake pedal while trying to park. The air blast coming off the hood is what tossed me out of my chair. If the undercarriage of the car had not caught up on the steel rebar holding the window frame to the ground level brickwork, I would have been run over and probably killed.

The car wasn't particularly damaged confirming what I had always heard about Volvos being built like tanks. Incredibly the police were comforting the girl who did not even receive a ticket after destroying the restaurant and nearly killing two lawyers! We returned to courthouse covered in dust and glass fragments. The Judge was very upset to hear about the restaurant damage as it was a favorite hangout for the court staff. We did manage to resolve our case before I drove myself to the hospital.

I decided then that if I could die just having a cup of coffee while sitting in a restaurant, why not learn to ride a motorcycle safely? My Dad came on board to the idea first and then my mother.

Dad pointed out that in World War Two he made it through four years of combat safely while others were killed on their first day. When it is your time to die it doesn't matter where you are or what you are doing.

I took a California Highway Patrol class on motorcycle operation and safety. Soon I got my motorcycle operator's license.

I sued my auto insurance carrier for uninsured motorist damages. My agent pointed put that I was not in a car when injured. I asked him to show me where my policy excluded this situation from coverage?

I used the settlement from the injury to buy a Harley Davidson Heritage Softail Springer in dark cobalt blue and silver metallic paint. When you ride, it feels like you are flying on the bridge of the Starship Enterprise headed home. The roar of the V Twin engine, the instant response of the machine, it is joyful to ride.

I could smell the flowers of gardens as I rode past them. I learned that you can smell the rain several minutes before riding into it. The camaraderie of other bikers, trips along the coast or out of state, there is nothing really comparable.

Sheryl and I dated on that bike. On our honeymoon in Maui we rented a black Harley Heritage Softail and rode together up the Haleakala volcano. Our engagement photo was taken with my Harley in the picture. I have had other motorcycles since then but none that have touched my heart like that first motorcycle. In retrospect, that leg and back injury was the best thing that could have happened to me. It prompted me to pursue a dream that has added immense joy to my life. Within reason, take some chances, pursue your goals and dreams.

Most importantly, do and say things that will leave behind good memories for others. Thank God daily for your life, no matter what it is like, and pray to be useful each day. Know that when it is time to be called home to God, overwhelming joy ultimately is waiting for you in God's blazing and eternal Light.

Lekh B'Shalom, (Go forward in peace)

Rabbi Gary M. Spero

July 27, 2014